Faith Restored

"A Pakistani Women's Journey from Land of Islam to a Nation under God' a Christian Perspective

Orpha James

MS Plastics Engineering
MS Biotechnology
BSc. Chemistry & Physics
B.Ed. Teaching of Science

WESTBOW
PRESS
A DIVISION OF THOMAS NELSON
& ZONDERVAN

WestBow Press books may be ordered through booksellers or by contacting:

WestBow Press
A Division of Thomas Nelson & Zondervan
1663 Liberty Drive
Bloomington, IN 47403
www.westbowpress.com
844-714-3454

ISBN: 978-1-6642-8701-3 (sc)
ISBN: 978-1-6642-8703-7 (hc)
ISBN: 978-1-6642-8702-0 (e)

Library of Congress Control Number: 2022923295

Print information available on the last page.

WestBow Press rev. date: 12/22/2022

CONTENTS

INTRODUCTION

This memoir is for anyone, anywhere in the world, who has pain for people who suffer religious persecution, race persecution, gender persecution and color persecution. It is hurtful and painful it seems like no one is listening and you are crying at the bottom of the well and there is no hope to get out.

I decided to write this book and tell my story to the world as persecution is at its peak in Pakistan. I felt deep sadness, when I was prosecuted as a little girl being a Christian, when a school near my home did not give me admission due to my religion in Pakistan that left a scar. I wanted to go to the PAF school, which was at the end of the block where, I lived but they refused they could not provide me the catechism or history since every girl over there was Muslim. Although my father was an ex-air force man. Acronym PAF stands for Pakistan Airforce. This school was built for air force employee's children at that time. Growing up in a Muslim country was very difficult. Each step of life was hard and harder. I always wonder why I was born in a Christian home what was the purpose. Now when I am a senior, I realized that there must be a reason why God put me in a Christian home. My faith is strong. I am seeing there is a problem in the world in the country, I lived before and the country I am living in now. Isn't it the same problem? With this Covid_19 and the riots in USA, the BML has given me enough cause to pen it down. However, some folks in my life have advised me to write a book on these issues and specially on the travels I do. I thought when I will retire; I will have some time to write. Covid_19 has given me some down time to write now, not later this is the time. No one knows how long this pandemic will last. I am not retired at present but not travelling like I use to do, every week I was flying to different states or countries.

I know I cannot solve the problem of the entire universe, but I can contribute and make awareness that persecution is a problem. How can we resolve this problem?

In Luke, **Jesus** speaks of "people [who] hate" and "defame you on account of the Son of Man" and likens his followers' suffering to that of earlier prophets (Luke 6:22-23 NIV). **Jesus** later **says** to "not fear those who kill the body and after that can **do** nothing more" (Luke 12:4 NIV).

When Christianity started persecution of Christians started at the same time. The Christians in the early church suffered great persecution and martyrdom. First person persecuted was "Stephen". Then others were persecuted namely James. All twelve Apostles were persecuted and martyred, except for John, and they died an excruciating death.

How can we resolve this issue of persecution in Pakistan? I know persecution is everywhere in the world but the most persecuted Christians in the world, are the Pakistani Christian People. You will ask me why? It is due to the Pakistani Blasphemy Laws. I will describe this in Chapter II why I am saying that. Pakistan is Muslim Country, but its sharia laws and blasphemy laws are most stringent than any Muslim Country in this world. I have spoken to the Senators in my state, such as Scott Brown when he was the senator, and so, they do hear my story. How can we make Pakistan change its laws how many people must die because they are Christian?

I have noticed in more than forty years living in US. That whenever there is a republican president In US than Pakistan it is little calm & peaceful in, as well as in southeast Asia, some might agree or disagree with me. But bringing a republican president is not a solution to this issue. Either UN or any other world organization must help the persecuted Christians to live peaceful life in that country. Or US must stop giving any aid or have put sanctions to stop persecution of Christian and in this way, Pakistan can change the sharia law & blasphemy law. I have seen a lot of changes in the countries where US has put sanctions.

This should be done sooner than later as the riots and kidnapping of young girls is at the peak now.

I want to request the parents and people who are raising young girls & children in Pakistan be on vigilance. Prepare your children right from the beginning as bible states. Proverb 26.6 [NIV]Train up a child in the way he should go: and when he is old, he will not depart from it.

This story is my story as well the move from Pakistan to US journey of Life. "A Pakistani Women's Journey from Land of Islam to a nation under God a Christian Perspective".

Text: Matthew 5:10–12 [NIV]

10 Blessed are those who are persecuted because of righteousness,

for theirs is the kingdom of heaven.

11 "Blessed are you when people insult you, persecute you and falsely say all kinds of evil against you because of me.

12 Rejoice and be glad, because great is your reward in heaven, for in the same way they persecuted the prophets who were before you.

As far as talking about respect for women, the only one I know who respected women was "**Jesus**", no other mankind in history respected women as much as Jesus did.

CHAPTER I
History of Pakistan

It is always good to learn about the history of the country where there are religious problems. The origin of a country, and its culture. Pakistan was a part of India. In this chapter, I will write a short history of Pakistan.

Religions of India

There were many religions in India however, the three main religious groups were Hindus, Muslims, and Christians.

The Hindus were in India. Hinduism is believed to be the world's oldest religion, according to scholars. Its roots and customs date back more than four thousand years. The oldest Hindu religions are the three *isms*: Hinduism, Buddhism, and Jainism. The three religions share the same beliefs about reincarnation, karma, liberation, and nirvana.

How Muslims Came to India

Muslims first came to India in the eighth century for trade and commerce from the Malabar Coast. Arabs conquered extensive territories from AD 711–713 under Muhammad-Bin-Qasim. [https://www.mapsofindia.com/history/battles/arab-invasion-of-sind-under-mohammed-bin-qasim.html]

How Christians Came to India

When one of Jesus's apostle, Thomas, supposedly reached the Malabar Coast (Kerala) in AD 52, although no written works exist from this period. It is word of mouth and believed that several different churches exist with several different traditions. Apostle Thomas succeeded in converting local Indians to Christianity. His converts were called Syrian Christians. Thomas' grave is still in India people go to pay homage.

Later, other Christians arrived in India as missionaries. It has been estimated that more Indians were converted to Christianity by European missionaries around the fifteenth century.[1]

Prior to 1947, India and Pakistan were one country. It was called India. The British ruled in India from 1858 through 1947.

Why India and Pakistan were Divided

In the first half of the nineteenth century, the Indian subcontinent was appropriated by the East India Company Britishers came as traders. Around 1857, they ruled India for the next ninety years. The religions in that region were predominantly Hindu and Muslim. Divisions between Hindus and Muslims had been encouraged by the British "divide and rule" approach.

There were several mutinies within the British army, which was comprised of mostly locals. There were religious issues raised among the Hindus and Muslims. It was difficult for the British to rule India. Hindus wanted their own state, "Hindustan," and Muslims wanted their own state. Chaudhary Rehmat Ali was the first to conceive of the idea of Pakistan: a free Islamic society and an independent state.

For the Hindus of India, Gandhi became the leader for independence in 1921. The incidents in Jallianwala Bagh spurred him into taking a larger role in the freedom fight. Gandhi believed in nonviolence and started the noncooperation movement to urge Indians to boycott British goods.

World War II (1939–45) was a major turning point for the British rule, as there were growing movements for independence. When Sir Winston Churchill asked the Indians to join World War II, Gandhi launched the Quit India Movement in 1942, refusing to cooperate with the British during the war until India gained independence.

The British announced the partition into two nations: India and Pakistan. This announcement came after unrest in the country between Hindus and Muslims. However, Gandhi believed in unity but was unable to stop the partition. Gandhi called for the two religious groups to work together, and the leader of the political group the Muslim League, Muhammad Ali Jinnah, believed that Muslims needed a homeland within India. It was decided that most of the Hindu area will be Hindustan and Muslim areas would be Pakistan. Some areas were given right to choose while others were divided up. The three main provinces, Assam, Bengal, and Punjab were divided. A British lawyer, Cyril Radcliffe, who had never traveled to India, was asked to draw the border lines between the two countries within five days. Thus, Pakistan came to independence on August 14, 1947, whereas India gained its independence from the British rule on August 15, 1947. Approximately two million lives were lost, and approximately fourteen million refugees were shifted within the two countries. It was estimated that approximately seven million Hindus and Sikhs and seven million Muslims found themselves in the wrong country.

Mohammed Ali Jinnah became the first governor-general of Pakistan, and Jawaharlal Nehru became India's first president. Gandhi was shot by a Hindu religious fanatic in 1948, just one month before the British last troops were about to leave India.

Sometimes I wonder why Christians were in Pakistan. Did they support the making of Pakistan? With a little research, I found that, yes, Christians did very much support the making of Pakistan.

How Christians Supported the Making of Pakistan

While I was researching why Christians came to Pakistan or supported Pakistan, I discovered that

> "[the Christians strongly supported Quaid-e-Azam and the Muslim League at that critical time when there was lot of opposition to the formation a new Muslim state. The All-India Christian Association assured unconditional, full cooperation to the founder of Pakistan. This crucial role of the Christian population of the region was recognized by the founder of Pakistan and the All-India Muslim League at all levels. These Christians played a very strong role in the creation of Pakistan. The leaders of the All-India Muslim League promised to give more privileges to the minorities, especially to Christian community, in the newly established Muslim state. The Christian vote before the Boundary Commission was the only decisive vote for the true foundation of Pakistan. Christian leaders voted for Pakistan because they believed that Quaid-e-Azam would be the real protector of their rights and interests.

Apart from the establishment of the Indian National Congress, many Christian leaders put their efforts into the deliberation and activities of the freedom movement. Sir Joseph Burr was the member of the viceroy's council and advisor of the Nawab of Bhopal. Mr. Paythan Joseph was the editor of the *Hindustan Times*, and B. G. Harmony edited the *Daily Dawn*. Being a friend of Mr. Jinnah, he supported the Muslim cause, and for these activities he was exiled for five years. Sir Samuel Ranganadhar, while serving as high commissioner in London, had close ties with Mr. Jinnah.

The All-India Christian Association was established by Dewan Bahadur S. P. Singha in 1942. This association contributed a lot to the effort and deliberation of the freedom movement. On November 18, 1942, at the annual convention of the All-India Muslim League, Punjab convened in Faisalabad (then Lyall Pur). It was attended by Mr. Jinnah and Miss Fatima. The All-India Christian Association presented a *spasnama* assuring its unconditional and full cooperation to Mr. Jinnah in connection with his efforts for the freedom of India.

When the general elections of 1946 were held in India, the Christians supported Mr. Jinnah and contested the election side by side with the Muslim League. Mr. Fazal Elahi and Dewan Bahadur S. P. Singha were elected to the Punjab Legislative Assembly. After achieving substantial success in the 1945–46 election. Moreover, due to these three Christian leaders, Mr. Fazal Elahi (a Christian) and Dewan Bahadur (a Christian), S. P. Singha [A Christian], Punjab was liberated to Pakistan. There were eighty-eight votes, and along with these three Christian votes, the total came to ninety-one. That is how Punjab became part of Pakistan.]"[2]

The Story of Pakistan

At the time of division, there were two major Muslim populated areas in India separated by 1000 miles within India therefor they became West and East Pakistan.

It seems like all Pakistanis are same, but that is not true. Although West and East Pakistan were Muslim-majority areas, they were culturally, ethnically, and linguistically very different people.

In 1971, East Pakistan fought for independence and was backed by Indira Gandhi, who was then the Indian prime minister. The two-week Indo-Pakistani War was fought in early December 1971, and on December 16 (about nine months after the conflict in East Pakistan), West Pakistan lost East Pakistan. East Pakistan became Bangladesh, meaning "land of the Bengalis," was born after this war.

Since these East and West Pakistan were thousand miles apart, they couldn't establish the unity among themselves, and India took advantage to divide the already separated country into the new country of Bangladesh.

"[Pakistan officially is the Islamic Republic of Pakistan, a country in South Asia. It is the world's fifth-most populous country with a population exceeding 212.2 million and has the world's second-largest Muslim population. Pakistan is the thirty-third-largest country by area, spanning 881,913 square kilometers.]"[3]

Population of Pakistan

According to the 2017 census, Muslims make up 96.2 percent of Pakistan's population; Hindus, 1.6 percent; Christians, 1.59 percent; scheduled castes, 0.25 percent; Ahmadis, 0.22 percent; and other minorities, 0.07 percent. [4]

Population of Christians in Pakistan

Christians and Hindus make up the two major religious minorities in Pakistan. The total number of Christians in Pakistan was estimated 4.0 million in 2020, or 2 percent of the population, during the census. Half of the Christians are Catholic, and half are Protestant. A small number of Eastern Orthodox Christians also live in Pakistan. Seventy-five percent of Pakistan's Christians are Punjabi. [5]

---

a. Islamic Law and Religious Persecution

Persecution versus Discrimination

Persecution derives from the Greek word for "persecute," *dioko* (διώκω), which literally means "to pursue, to put to flight, or to chase after".[5] In a positive sense, it can mean to eagerly pursue or seek something. However, in a negative sense, it means to pursue with an intent to harm. Thus, by implication it means "hostility and ill-treatment, especially because of race or political or religious beliefs"—hence, to persecute.[6]

Discrimination means unfair or prejudicial treatment of different categories of people or things, especially on the grounds of race, age, or sex.

By comparing these two words, I will be using persecution based on the religious or political belief throughout this book.

Pakistan is the only country where Christians and minorities are persecuted more than anywhere else in the world.

The reason is that this is the only country where the blasphemy law is implemented. The Pakistan Penal Code, the main criminal code of Pakistan, punishes blasphemy against any recognized religion, providing penalties ranging from a fine to death.[7]

The Pakistan Penal Code, abbreviated as PPC, is a penal code for all offences charged in Pakistan. It was originally prepared by Lord Macaulay with a great consultation in 1860 on the behalf of the Government of India as the Indian Penal Code. After the independence in 1947, Pakistan inherited the same code and subsequently after several amendments by different governments, in Pakistan it is now a mixture of Islamic and English Law. Presently, the Pakistan Penal Code is still in effect and can be amended by the Senate of Pakistan.

Blasphemy laws are commonly used around the world to persecute people for beliefs and activities that do not conform to the majority opinion on religious and sensitive topics, and to suppress criticism of religion. They have been subject to repeated condemnations by human rights organizations and resolutions of the United Nations Human Rights Council. In some parts of the world, blasphemy laws on statute books have not been enforced for many years, but a concerted international campaign since 2015 has sought to repeal these laws in with the hope of further drawing attention to the way these laws are used around the world to persecute religious and political minorities.

Background of Blasphemy Law:

The offences relating to religion were first codified by India's British rulers in 1860 and were expanded in 1927. Pakistan inherited these laws when it came into existence after the partition of India in 1947.

Around early 80's, several clauses were added to the laws that made the Ahmadi community, outcast as not Muslims. Although Ahmadi community calls themselves muslins.[2]

Pakistan's blasphemy laws carry a potential death sentence for anyone who insults Islam. Critics say they have been used to persecute minority faiths and unfairly target minorities.

The law enacted by the British made it a crime to disturb a religious assembly, trespass on burial grounds, insult religious beliefs or intentionally destroy or defile a place or an object of worship. The maximum punishment under these laws ranges from one year to 10 years in jail, with or without a fine.

During the 1980s the blasphemy laws were created and expanded in several installments. In 1980, making derogatory remarks against Islamic personages was made an offence, carrying a maximum punishment of three years in jail.

There were two laws made:

295-B, defiling the Holy Quran

295-C: use of derogatory remarks etc., in respect of the Holy Prophet

Defiling the copy of Holy Quran. Whoever willfully defiles, damages, or desecrates a copy of the Holy Quran or of an extract there from or uses it in any derogatory manner for any unlawful purpose shall be punishable with imprisonment for life.

The law stipulated death penalty or life imprisonment for defiling the name of the prophet of Islam.

The above laws seem to protect the of faith of only one community in a multifaith society, whereas that community is already in majority and ruling class of the country they live in. On the contrary these laws provide no protection to members of other religions and hence they are discriminatory. They are used against the members of other religious communities including Christians, Ahmadis, and Hindus and even against Muslims who have some differences with main sects.

Christians are the main targets by the fundamentalist and religious political parties. The law is being used in forced conversion, forcibly taking over the lands and business of Christians, hindering the preaching of Christian faith and for settling personal scores. Nevertheless, these laws have proved to be the most injurious weapon of active religious persecution by the extremists.

At present the majority of Christians in Pakistan belong to the lower economic status of society.

Mostly, blasphemy cases are either brought by those wishing to undermine minority groups or by those wishing to eliminate individuals against whom they have a feud or grudge. The mere accusation of blasphemy against someone can result in the accused's life being endangered.

Below are the stories which I have followed during these times. however, there is one story in each household about the prosecution.

One Little Christian Boy:

I believe that if this little boy was not Christian, he would be alive at this time. In 1995 he was murdered he raised voice against child labor.

The reason was because he raised voice against the child labor that little boy was murdered. My opinion on this case was that he was Christian and got attention of the world.

A Christian Women:

The second case which made the world news was a Christian woman, the allegations against her, when Muslim laborer's working with her in the fields refused to share their water because she was a Christian.

An argument broke out and a woman went to a local cleric to accuse her of committing blasphemy. She was sentenced to death This was one of the several cases like this.

A Minister:

On 2 March 2011, member of the cabinet and the minister for Minorities, was shot dead outside his mother's house. He was the only senior Pakistani official

He dedicated his life to empower the minorities specially Christians. He united several platforms and trying to change the blasphemy law. During his tenor he proposed to ban hate speech and related literature. He was successful in proposing the four religious minority senate seats. He was against terrorism he headed up interfaith consultation organization, which brought the religious leaders on one platform.

125 family's homes were burnt due to blasphemy law this incident happened:

Please see the entire news in the following website.

125 Christian houses burnt over blasphemy - Pakistan - DAWN.COM

There have been incidences where the families are burnt alive being accused of desecrating the Muslim holy book. This was a heartfelt issue for me I asked our family friend who was the DSP at that time can you ask the folks I want to adopt the children who are left behind. This conversation did not go further as too much was going on in that country at the time.

2020 was another challenging year for Christians in Pakistan, as the country entered a national lockdown in March to thwart the spread of the novel COVID_19 virus. The country's poor and marginalized communities (which many Christians were a part of) were severely affected by disruption. The International Christian Concern (ICC) documented at least 80 incidents of persecution against Pakistan's Christian population within the first 6 months of 2020, including at least 12 incidents in which Christians were denied food.

If you need to read more about these incidences, please go to the following website.

https://www.aninews.in/news/world/asia/pakistan-christian-nurse-beaten-by-her-muslim-colleagues-after-accusing-her-of-blasphemy20210214145045/

Pakistan: Christian nurse beaten by her Muslim colleagues Jan 2021

More recently Christian nurse was beaten at her job. There was a rumor that she was speaking against prophet. She just said to a patient that she would pray for her, as she was going into labor, and it was her first child. That is when everything started – the nurses who were there pounced on her. She was trying her best to save herself, she went from room to room, and locked herself in, but they climbed through the window to open the door. Once they opened the door, they asked the women to go and beat her; they dragged her from the third to the ground floor on the stairs. A local chaplain said the incident was "pre-planned" and followed several months of tension between her and her colleagues, who had asked her to leave her job and get transferred to another hospital. She was being charge 295-C blasphemy Law.

I have received more persecution cases information sent to me by my cousin from local police stations from Punjab area.

Amnesty International has repeatedly asked the Government of Pakistan to abolish the Blasphemy Law and provide protection to Pakistan's Shias,

Ahmadis, Christians, Hindus Zoroastrians and other minorities. Section 295 C of the Pakistan Penal Code which mandates the death penalty for crimes of Blasphemy must urgently be repealed to prevent the further bullying of innocent Pakistani citizens at the hands of religious extremists.

Girls are abducted:

On September 3, 2020, a petition was filed by, a 15-year-old Christian girl who was abducted almost a full year ago in a province of Pakistan. Despite attempts by her family to pursue her freedom in Pakistani courts, she remains in the custody of her abductors.

In October of 2019, a man commonly hired by the man's family for transportation purposes, kidnapped her at gunpoint, who was 14 years old at the time. In the following days, her parents, received WhatsApp messages from his brother. The messages showed a series of documents, showing that she had been forcibly married to a man and converted to Islam. Upon further examination, these documents had clearly been falsified, listing her as 18 years old to justify the marriage.

The parents filed a case in Pakistani courts to try and gain girls, freedom and have her returned. As a result, they received death threats, coming in the form of videos depicting, using threatening language while firing guns. Nevertheless, her parents continued to pursue legal action with little success.

In an early ruling, the local court validated her marriage to man, citing Islamic laws allowing marriage after a girl has begun her menstrual cycles. This again is one of the many cases that takes place on a regular basis.

However, this law differs from Pakistani law. Specifically, the Sindh Child Marriage Restraint Act forbids marriage under the age of 18, clearly outlawing girls' marriage with the man. Moreover, this is not the only law that would invalidate the marriage. According to Section 365-B of the Pakistan Penal Code, any marriage which takes place between an abductor and an abductee is invalid. Girls' parents appealed the case, again with no success.

The latest persecution about seven-year-old case of another Christian the verdict was announced September 8, 2020. This Christian man was 37-year-old Pakistani Christian has been sentenced to death for allegedly sending blasphemous text messages in 2013. According to his attorney the death sentence was announced by the court despite there being 'no evidence' to implicate his client in the case.

In Pakistan, false accusations of blasphemy are widespread and often motivated by personal vendettas or religious hatred. Accusations are highly inflammatory and have the potential to spark mob lynching's, vigilante murders, and mass protests.

Currently, 25 Christian are imprisoned on blasphemy charges in Pakistan, including above Christian man. These 25 Christians are defendants in 22 blasphemy cases represented at various levels of the judicial process in Pakistan.

Child Marriage:

21% of girls in Pakistan are married before their 18th birthday and 3% are married before the age of 15. Pakistan has the sixth highest number of absolute child brides in the world.

The practice of child marriage is prevalent in Pakistan, with the highest prevalence in Sindh province. It disproportionately affects the girl child. Most recently the high court in Pakistan has ruled those men can **marry** underage girls, under Sharia **law**, after they have experienced their first menstrual cycle.

Sharia law is the religious law of Islam derived from the teachings of the Quran, which acts as a divine code or guide for living.

The ruling was made by the Sindh High Court during the hearing, a 14-year-old Catholic girl who was abducted, pressured to convert to Islam, and forced into child marriage. The parents are devasted and will appeal in the high court.

Child marriage is a major human rights violation, which causes irreparable harm to young girls all over the world.

Now a days it is sad, how Christian young girls are abducted by the Muslims in rural areas and Christian families are suffering and they have nowhere to go. Christian people in the villages are scared about this law.

The Church in Pakistan has also protested the similar cases of child marriages of forced marriages of young Christian girls.

According to a 2019 report by the human rights commission of Pakistan, an estimated 1,000 Christian and Hindu women are abducted and forcibly married every year. Many of the victims are minors. Sexual assaults and fraudulent marriages are used by perpetrators to entrap victims, and authorities rarely intervene.

Nearly 1,000 girls from religious minorities who are forced to convert to Islam in Pakistan each year, largely to pave the way for marriages that are under the legal age and non-consensual. Human rights activists say the practice has accelerated during lockdowns against the coronavirus, when girls are out of school and more visible, bride traffickers are more active on the Internet and families are more in debt.

The girls generally are kidnapped by complicit acquaintances and relatives or men looking for brides. Sometimes they are taken by powerful landlords as payment for outstanding debts by their farmhand parents, and police often look the other way. Once converted, the girls are quickly married off, often to older men or to their abductors, according to the independent Human Rights Commission of Pakistan.

Forced conversions thrive unchecked on a money-making web that involves Islamic clerics who solemnize the marriages, magistrates who legalize the unions and corrupt local police who aid the culprits by refusing to investigate or sabotaging investigations, say child protection activists.

Child marriage and conversion is becoming an issue in this country. We can pray for these families there should be a solution. The thought is how the laws in this country can be changed.

Abductions, sexual assaults, forced conversions and forced marriages also continue to affect Pakistan's Christian community in the second half of 2020.

There is a lot of information on the internet about this issue.

If I go on writing about these incidences, I will never be able to finish this book since it is a continuous process the Pakistani Authorities are not taking this issue seriously.

Forced conversion in exchange for aid.

Christians and other religious minorities were also pressured into converting to Islam to gain access to food aid, using COVID-19 food aid. There are several news surfacing in the medial "people who are exploiting the lockdown due to Covid-19, and the desperation created by so many poor people, to induce a religious conversion to Islam, an act of blackmail: if you want food, you must become a Muslim".

Since I started writing this book it has come to my knowledge through the social media the cases of forced marriages and abduction of young girls are becoming prevalent in that part of the world.

A lawyer in Pakistan talks about the well-known practice of "forced conversions" of Hindu and Christian girls to Islam, through forced marriages with Muslim men. The vulnerability of girls belonging to religious minorities has further increased with the outbreak of the global Covid_19 pandemic. There are recent cases of refusal of food and emergency aid to people of the Hindu and Christian communities. Covid_19 could offer an excuse to resort to the religious conversion of young women as a means of saving their life or their family in times of crisis. Once converted, a woman cannot go back, if they do that implies death sentence.

I started looking up the recent persecution cases in Pakistan. I found several cases which are still pending due to resources. One of cousin sent me some cases to review for this part of my book.

In most cases the victim is abducted and is then subjugated to sustained emotional and physical abuse often involving threats of violence towards their loved ones.

Many religious institutions, local mosques and seminaries fail to investigate the nature of the conversion or the age of the bride and mostly simply accept the word of the abductor and routinely encourage the practice of converting members of minority communities by offering rewards for successful conversions.

There are numerous protests going on however the law has not been changed. Each issue is treated case by case if we do not raise our voice on anyone that is a dead case goes into dead files and no one looks at it the person dies in jail or so.

Refugee Situation:

Due to unbearable situation majority of the Christians want to get out of Pakistan.

There are several examples of Pakistani Christians who want to seek asylum in European or other countries their applications have been denied.

Across the globe, in the Middle East, Asia and Africa, Christians are being bullied, arrested, jailed, expelled, and executed. Christianity is by most calculations the most persecuted religion of modern times. Yet Western politicians until now have been reluctant to speak out in support of Christians in peril.

Many persecuted Pakistani Christian asylum seekers are being denied refugee status and deported back to Pakistan where their lives remain 'at risk' because UK and UNHCR (the United Nations' Refugee Agency) decision makers are drawing upon this entirely misleading Home Office 'guidance' to arrive at their 'refugee status' determinations.

These <u>are the signs of times. His coming is soon.</u> The scriptures tell us that in the last days the Christ followers will be persecuted. Same way as the Jews and other nations did to Christ.

Matthew chapter 5 verse 11-12. (NJV)

[11] Blessed are ye, when men shall revile you, and persecute you, and shall say all manner of evil against you falsely, for my sake.

[12] Rejoice and be exceeding glad: for great is your reward in heaven: for so persecuted they the prophets which were before you.

Matthew 24:9[NIV]

9 "Then you will be handed over to be persecuted and put to death, and you will be hated by all nations because of me. 10 At that time many will turn away from the faith and will betray and hate each other.

Luke 6:22-23[NIV]

22 Blessed are you when people hate you, when they exclude you and insult you and reject your name as evil, because of the Son of Man.

23 "Rejoice in that day and leap for joy, because great is your reward in heaven. For that is how their ancestors treated the prophets.

The reason for giving these direct predictions is to strengthen faith. Believers should recognize that hardship is not something which catches God by surprise. Rather, this is exactly how He told us things would play out. In the previous verse, Christ pointed out that some of the most brutal oppression will come from those who think murdering Christians is an act of good!

One report did say that the laws can be changed. BBC world Asia reported that there were some agenda that,

Amending the blasphemy laws has been on the agenda of many popular secular parties. None has made much progress - principally because of the sensitivities over the issue, but also because no major party wants to antagonize the religious parties.[2]

https://www.bbc.com/news/world-asia-48204815

b. View of women in Islam

The *Quran* explicitly states that men and *women* are equal in the eyes of God. Also, Quran instruct that the women child should not be killed, educate girls, give right to women to divorce under certain conditions, women have the right to refuse a prospective husband, gives right to own and inherit property. While polygyny is permissible, it is discouraged and on the whole practices less frequently than imagined by the rest of the world.

It is interesting to note that the only one woman in the Holy Quran mentioned by name is Mary (Maryam). The others' names come from different traditions. Most of the women in the Quran are represented as either the mothers or wives of leaders or prophets. Mary the mother of Jesus name is mentioned in the New Testament but Quran it is exceeded. It has its own title Sura 19 which discuss the annunciation.

There are few subjects where I feel the women's have not too much freedom: Such as veil that covers the face.

Veil (hijab) is imposed on women in many countries under the influence of Islam, either legally or under cultural and social pressure.

During the last thirty years, hijab has been and continues to be the political and ideological symbol of political Islam, Islamic states and the Islamic movement in the Middle East, North Africa, and Central Asia. Saudi women typically don a billowy black cloak called an Abaya, along with a black scarf and veil over the face.

Choice of Marriage: although it is written in Quran that women have the right but what It has been observed in Pakistan it is not women's choice that matters, it the choice of parents or the society who picks a partner. There are 25-40% of marriages are arranged with first cousins in Pakistan and Saudi Arabia. Altogether 80% of marriages are arranged.

An arranged marriage can be described as a marriage wherein a person's bride or groom is purposefully selected by a third-party, most often by elder family members like parents and grandparents. Oftentimes a professional matchmaker is involved in the selection process. Some arranged marriages can be planned even while the bride and groom are still infants.

However, 90% percentage of arrange marriages are arranged in Pakistan. This again shows that the women do not have freedom of her choice.

While family law and personal status codes in Arab and Muslim countries restrict women's rights and freedoms (e.g., in choosing a husband, guardianship. obeying the husband, initiating divorce, dowry requirement, polygamy, marriage to non-Muslims, etc.).

I really do not want to go deep into the religion and the view of women in Pakistan being an Islamic Republic of Pakistan. Some women are highly educated they are doctors, teachers, engineers, and scientists.

c. Islam and Minority Children.

It came to my attention that on 24 September 2021, one of the high court rules non-Muslim children as young as 10 can convert to Islam. This is so strange scientifically human brain is not developed in size till the age of 14 how can a child decide of their religion or religious beliefs. The human brain adapts environments during the years of 14-25.

Read more at: https://www.southasiamonitor.org/pakistan/no-minimum-age-conversion-islam-says-pakistan-court-dismissing-christian-rickshaw-pullers

Interview with a Persecuted Christian

After reading and watching most of the stories of persecuted Christians. I Interviewed a Christian fellow who was given a political asylum in Western Country after staying as a refugee with five children and a wife. His story is mind boggling.

He said they were working in rural areas on medical mobiles. He and his team brought medical aids to these rural areas. This group performed medical treatment to the needy. Beside all this they were helping poor bringing food and money during Eid.

This was not appreciated by the Mulla's, so they attacked his group. He fled to another country as a refugee. During Covid_19. It was miracle for him and his family to move to a western country.

3 Ecclesiastes .1 There is a time for everything, and a season for every activity under the heavens (NIV).

https://www.facebook.com/pages/category/Local-Business/Console-Human-Rights-IntL-Trust-1569545449857478/

There are several other Christians facing persecution. However, if we go into the early church, they also faced persecution.

Persecution in the Early Church

Persecution and suffering are listed as throughout the Bible. The word persecution occurs 45 times in the New Testament. All of Jesus disciples were persecuted in form or another and is documented in the New Testament. Hebrews, Philippians, and the first Peter among them. Many of Paul's letters were written from prison, where he was confined because of his gospel preaching: Philippians, Ephesians, Colossians, and Philemon. John received the Revelation while banished to Patmos, essentially an island prison colony.

Just to make it clear Jesus had 12 disciples. It is interesting to know how 12 apostles died, but the New Testament tells of the fate of only two of the apostles: Judas, who betrayed Jesus and then went out and hanged himself, and James the son of Zebedee, who was executed by Herod about 44 AD. (Acts 12:2). He had James, the brother of John, put to death with the sword.

There is always a question in my head if there were 12 disciples what happened after Judas. 12, which some scholars interpret as a reference to the 12 tribes of Israel. When a gap had been left by the defection and death of the traitor Judas Iscariot, immediate steps were taken to fill it by the election of Matthias (Acts 1).

We cannot stop persecution however we can pray for His people to be safe. We can bring awareness to the world so may be one day it can end.

CHAPTER II
Growing up in Pakistan

---

a. Early Childhood (relationship with mother and father; father's rules)

Living in a Muslim country as a Christian was not that easy to begin with, let alone growing up as a female moreover being born into a Christian family in Pakistan was not easy. We were a middle-class working family. My "ABA" (father) worked in the Pakistan International Airforce, in the mechanical engineering department. He moved from India during the partition of India and Pakistan when his Indian air force plane landed in Karachi. The Indian Air force becomes the Pakistan Airforce. My father studied aeronautical engineering at DAV college in Punjab, India and my mother was at the mission high school. They were engaged in India prior to my father's arrival to Karachi, Pakistan. At the time of the Partition in 1947, my mother could not come to meet my father in person. She was still in school in India and moved to Pakistan in 1949.

My father's parents were Christian since ages and the word of mouth is that they were Christians since Apostle Thomas came to India to spread the Gospel of Christ. My mother's mothers' mother was Hindu and specially I know my grandmother who raised me she uses to tell us all the stories of old India she was from a rich Hindu family, and they had a big, huge house in Shanti Negar in India at that time, my grandfather who owned many acre of farmland when he saw this young beautiful girl he fell in love with her. My grandfather was a good Christian man he was affiliated with salvation army church.

During the partition of India and Pakistan my father was in air India and the airplane landed in Pakistan he stayed in Pakistan whereas he was engaged to my mother who was in still India.

In 1949 my mother moved to Pakistan my parents were married shortly thereafter. My father was 23 and my mother was 17. My grandfather (mothers father died prior to 1949) only my grandmother was left, my mother being the youngest child wanted my grandmother to live with my parents in Karachi. My parents had one daughter in 1951 who died within 9 months after the birth due to typhoid. Then my parents had three more children. If we count first daughter, then I was my parent's third child. I have an older brother and a younger brother when we moved to Peshawar.

I was born in Karachi the cosmopolitan city and the largest city of Pakistan. We had to move from Karachi as my Aba was posted to Peshawar. I do not remember the transfer since I was a baby at that time. My parent along with my grandma moved to Peshawar.

Our stay in Peshawar.

Peshawar Subdivision formerly Frontier Region Peshawar is a subdivision in Khyber Pakhtunkhwa province of Pakistan. The region is named after Peshawar district which lies to the north and west and borders Nowshera District to the east and Kohat Subdivision to the south the area Is 83 miles long and high elevation makes it a cold city. Peshawar was likely established as a village in the 5th-6th century BC (15).

Peshawar has different vegetation compared to Karachi. It had different fruits and vegetables mostly people were fair with blue eyes since it was a mountain area the elevation was 1086'. This city is famous for, food its traditional recipes include chapli **kebab**, fried fish and a rice-based dish with meat and raisins and caramelized carrots known as Kabuli pulao top the list. It is a beautiful city it was called the city of flowers until ten years ago.

My Aba was stationed in Peshawar while working for Pakistan Airforce. My mother taught at Saint Michael school. That was my first school. My parents had, three more children in Peshawar. All together we are six siblings four boys and two girls. My mother started preaching bible in the rural area Peshawar. All I remember she will be taking a Tonga horse riding and the Tonga man will ask her if he can cover Tonga, he wants to wrap a sheet around the Tonga so no one cannot see her she was very much respected in that area teachers are respected a lot in that part of the world. In the late 50's the women cannot be seen bare face but my mother being Christian, so it was not mandatory to wear the Niqab or Hijab. She will be teaching bible studies to the women who stayed home. My mother had a passion for Christianity. I have vivid memories when Rev. Bill Graham came to Peshawar and how my mother will wrap us in warm clothing to attend his service in the evening. Those evenings were cold and crisp. I somehow remember Billy Graham's name as the conversation about him happened often in our household. My parents never missed a church service. In those days the household chores were performed by the servants and my grandmother will watch us while my mother will go for missionary work.

My mother was math teacher, but she also taught sewing to young girls. Below is the picture of me at age 6 learning sewing in fourth grade. She moved to Seventh day Adventist school, and we went to this school was mostly American students as far I recall very small classrooms may be four students in one class.

Most of the students were the children of air force officer the air force area was nearby, and air force barracks were nearby as well.

My primary education was in catholic school, St. Michael in Peshawar, and then in Seventh Day Adventist School. The catholic schools were built by the Britishers who ruled India.

Life In Karachi:

In the early 60's we moved to Karachi and my father took an early retirement from his Air Force Job and went to work as a manager in a Hospital in Karachi. My mother started teaching in the nearby school. My father was given a twelve-room house, it seems like a mansion, and my siblings and I lived our daily lives happily, climbing on the almond trees and playing in the big yard in the gated community.

I still remember the day President Kennedy was assassinated. We were at church on Sabbath, and all-American people in the church started crying. I cried too, while walking out the church everyone was crying. Here I want to add the American folks who were attending the church were the doctors and nurses who were working in the hospital and attached was the church and school. This was in November 1963; I was in class 5. I felt saddened by this incident I did not knew who President Kennedy was at that time.

Somehow the job was not for my father. It did not work out and we had to move after staying in PECHS we moved to Drigh Road. The house which we moved in was a big house with seven bedrooms and a veranda and yard where my mother planted papaya tree. We had to change our schools in this area. My brothers were sent to distant English Medium catholic school. My father thought it was too much walk for me they put me in nearby school which was an Urdu Medium Catholic school.

My parents were very strict in raising us. Every Sunday morning, we must go to church and every evening we had a prayer at our home. My aba will be calling us at 6.am knocking at our bedrooms doors to get ready and however the church started at 10.00 am first the Sunday school and then the church service. It was hard getting up so early. My father was the superintendent of the Sunday school volunteer base while working with the Pakistan International Airlines. My mother was a schoolteacher she taught Math to the high school she also taught English as a second language to the primary school beside that she was also involved in the women society of Methodist church she was the president she will have monthly prayer meetings at different home this Women's group was so much involve in the bringing younger generation to the Christ.

I will be joining my mother all the time when she will be hosting the women society meetings. My job was to cook pakora or chana chat for the ladies and make tea. Then I will be sitting with them in the prayer meetings. This prayer meeting was weekly prayers at someone house or at house. This group was called United Methodist Women group.

The Methodist church was a living church. In those days we were very happy. We had a choir, Easter pageant Christmas drama and the caroling on Christmas eve was the fun part of all. The children we will be singing and caroling at the Christian homes they will give us snacks and tea which clears our throat so we can move to next home. Easter pageant was early morning at the sunrise service. We had an Easter Morning procession in the town of Drigh Road wherever the Christian community lived we will be singing and praising that he is risen. These hymns still echo in my ears. This was a ritual we use to get up at 4.00 am to go to this procession. Tis procession goes through the empty roads in Drigh road singing on ward Christian solders and Jesus is resin from the grave. I became very much involve in the religion. I accepted Jesus Christ as my savior when I was 12 years of age. I still remember during the confirmation class I felt holy spirt has touched me and my entire life is changed. I felt very different then rest of the crowed, I read the entire bible in Urdu just to know what this religion is, reading was my passion at that age. Now I think back how I did that maybe it was just reading now I understand better, I am wiser now.

My Father (ABA) was involved in the Gideon Ministry in this ministry the bibles are placed in the hotels, schools, and prisons.

The Gideons International is an evangelical Christian association founded in 1899 in Wisconsin. The organization was founded by two travelling salesmen with a heart for evangelism they were talking about religion and found out they need the bible while travelling later they adapted the goal of putting Bible in every hotel room in United States starting in 1908. From those beginnings grew an organization of over 300,000 men and women in 195 countries giving out Bibles or New Testaments in over ninety languages. In their first 105 years, the Gideons have given out over 1.8 billion copies of God's Word.

b. teenage years, education, discrimination, or persecution; being a girl.

First Persecution

After going to the 8th grade in the Catholic school my father wanted me to carry my education in the girl's school, the closest school was a girls' school nearby this was not even a block from my home. This school was run by the government and air force at that time and being my father in the air force their chances I can get into this school. When my father and I went to admission office they refused to take me the reason was that I will be the only Christian girl and they cannot provide me catechism. I was very much disappointed I was 13-year-old at that time and the brain is not fully developed at the age 13-14 however it still has effects.

So, I ended up going to Methodist Secondary School it was co-ed school for both boys and girls. My father wanted us to learn Dinyaat in the school system. This is the subject that Muslim student take as an elective. The Christian or Hindus or other religions can take history in high school. My father had a theory behind it that if we are taking history the school board judges that this is a non-Muslim, so the grades are lowered.

My father advised all my siblings to take dinyaat as subject Muslims teach instead of catechism or history in high school. At the board exam mostly, Candidates were judged by the region, Muslim's student were allotted higher grades then the others another discrimination. All my sibling and I graduated high school with first division. We all were good in math and science as both my parents guided us during the high school. This was the only reason my brothers and sister passed their high school with first division. When my older brother my result for Metric came out we did not know until my father came from his work on the bicycle with the newspaper in his hand was dancing in the veranda still remember that good time vivid memories. We were a popular family in our town getting first division in school.

In Pakistan the school system is a British school system the high school is at ten classes then higher education school is two more years in a college and the two more years college you can earn a BSc or B.A degree. Then two years you have to the University and get your MA or MS degrees. It is slightly different now in Pakistan. The University of Karachi has semester system and the four years to do a BS degree.

Second Persecution on religion:

After passing the high school I went to higher education Allamah Iqbal College for FSc. It was a girl's college at that time near the Karachi airport. I sent to college with my friend every day she will come to my home then we will go to the bus stop and take the public bus to the college. In those days we cannot walk alone we have to go to school or college with some friend. In that college I ran for election student vice president for science. My opponent knew that I was Christian when we had debate for election she said if you want to give your vote to the non-religious person. However, students at time did not get it that my opponent is mentioning Christian faith, since my name is also recognized in Arabic and my last name was local in Urdu my name is spelled like an Arabic name. I won the election and became the vice president of the college. It was my first success in the college it became a news item in the newspaper in those days.

Elected Vice President of Allamah Iqbal College Karachi

In those days' women did not go to engineering college. My father went to Peshawar King Edwards College for my admission to become a doctor however that idea failed since Peshawar was 1000 miles from Karachi and they did not want me to study that far. I could not get admission in Karachi as there were only limited seats in the Medical or Engineering College for minorities. I persuaded my education in Chemistry and Biology in PECHS College all Women's college. At that, age I was full of energy I published an article about Christianity. I do not have any copy of that article it was in Jung Newspaper all I can remember that few news reporters came to my home and asked my father that we want her to write for this paper. My father refused and said we are very private people we do not want our daughter to write in a paper or journal. Later I came to know that they offered me to write the article they thought I was Muslim and writing about Christianity. My name can be Muslim, but it is spelled different it is like Arfa. However, in Urdu language they did not care if its Arfa or Orpha.

I completed my degree in BSc in PECHS college I wanted to pursue my education, but I was stopped because of the girl child. One of my teachers from Methodist School came and talked to my father I was listening he said to my father Mr. Bhatty, why you want to send Orpha to the University it will be hard to find a match for girls that that have higher education. My father told me not to pursue the University Studies. My Interest was in the marine biology at that time we were filling the admission papers at that time there was one University in Karachi. However, I stopped and stayed home without going to the further my education. While I was staying home, I was actively looking for a position in the pharmaceutical industry.

Third Persecution:

The first regular job I got, nearby pharmaceutical company. The van use to come and pick employees in my area I was very happy. All the staff was Muslim. One day I wore cross earing, my parents, brought from UK for me. I was let go of wearing the crosses, from my job. I was too young to ask him any question, what is the reason of this lay off only one person was laid off. I worked there only one week. Usually when you fill in the job application you must disclose your religion in Pakistan however my name sounded like Muslim somehow this application was overlooked.

I went to the American Language school in sadder Karachi downtown and did some courses in English and bible study course. Plus was very much involved in Campus Crusade of Christ at that time. We used to go to the roads and distribute Christian Literature at that time, there were people who will refuse to take but there were people who will take and read. I was also involved in the Campus Crusade of Christ the movement started by Bill Bright there were few members who were running this ministry in Drigh Road. We did the witnessing on the roads and gave brochure given to us by the ministry people will take those brochures. The main purpose was to spread the gospel. I am not sure if those brochures have ever converted any body into Christianity. There was no follow-up.

After this incidence my mother wanted me do teaching since she was a schoolteacher. It was difficult to get a job with no experience or I did not have a good luck. We believe in prayer I prayed and prayed. One Sunday one evangelist came to our church in Drigh road we asked him to pray for me he prayed with us, said just believe in God and it will be given few days later I looked in the newspaper and found a job.

Teaching:

I started teaching in a private school Chemistry at the same time, I went to college to get my education degree in teaching of Science and English. I used to go to college in the morning and teach in the second shift that is noon to five at Greenwood school. After I finished the college, I received a degree in Teaching of English as second Language and Teaching of Science B.Ed. In 1977 I traveled to US and Canada for a long vacation with my parents. My Aba used to work for PIA (Pakistan International Airline) so we get the free and discounted tickets to travel anywhere in the world. First American Embassy refused to give me a visa since I was too young and will never come back to Pakistan. My aba took me to Canadian Embassy and told him the story how American embassy has refused me the visa the visa officer said I will give her the visa for travel to Canada I don't care if America has refused her. In the interim I got a letter from the Methodist Church Convention in Mississippi my father has written the refusal story to the Pastor Amos Price he sent my parents including me the invitation to attend the convention. We took this letter to the American Embassy, and they saw that I already am going to Canada with my parents had a visa, so they gave me a visa based on the church letter. Every step God has helped me in my life.

This travel was eye opening when we went to Mississippi in the pastor announced that we are visitors from Pakistan. He said to welcome us by shaking hands while we stand some folks did not want to shake hands with us some did not want to talk to us it was due to our skin color. We should have known better in South they folks do not like foreigners in those days. However, there were some folks who made food for us and left at the pastor's house. Some invited us to their homes the convention was for a week at the banquet I wore my sky blue sharara (long skirt like dress covers to the ankles) which I had custom made for my older brothers' marriage. One of the girls, liked the sharara, I gave it to her. She got to excited and was very happy to wear it.

We stayed with my brother home in New Jersey his wife was expecting her first child. Then we went to Washington DC to see my father's friend from India and later we went to Canada and travelled back to US.

On my return I changed my school. I left Greenwood School and came to COD [Central Ordinance Depot] this was the army public school for teaching of science and math later my mother advised me to go to a government school where you will get pension and retirement and benefits. I applied for the government school and got the job at the same school where I graduated from high school. Drigh Road Methodist Secondary School. This was a great experience for me teaching to high school children. I still remember one student in ninth grade will bring me rose every morning for me and leave it on the table, now I think back where he was getting the flowers may be plucking from someone's yard. I found this job very respectful, and I enjoyed it. I know my students use to tell me that I was the best teacher. It brought my self-esteem high. While teaching I went to India to visit my aunty Alice in Dehra Doon along with my youngest brother whom we called Kukoo (nick name). He was very close to me and my sister, in his young age he uses to bring gift for me and sister. I know when he went to Quetta, he brought me purple suits these days I use to wear several suits and sarees for teaching. In teaching we have, to dress up, in the old country.

Girls Discrimination:

Being a girl child, I cannot go alone to any one's house there will be always an escort sent with me in those days. If a girl is shopping, she has a relative as a bodyguard. This was a precaution so one can abduct you. I remember one time one of my brothers, One of my brother pupo who was Judo Karate Instructor he had two dan [ranking system in karate] in Pakistan I have to go with him to my friend's party we were riding a motorcycle I was sitting behind him when a van of boy's gangsters started bullying and teasing me and my brother. He yelled at them and told them to stop they brought the van close to his motorcycle he told them to stop he put his motorcycle on the ground and told me to wait for his signal when he says run and jump, I should do that. The five men came out of there van near my brother and started swearing and started fist fight my brother being the karate champion he did his kicks and punched on one of the guys face I saw the front teeth came out to mouth and my brother picked up the motor bike asked me jump and we drove as fast as we can from that area this happened in the day light on share e Iraq.

I always had someone walking with me to the rail or bus stop my uncle called mamo or my nephew from my Uncle Mamo son mostly nephew will travel with me to downtown and my younger brother if I am going to another city or out of the country such as India.

Arrange Marriages:

Arrange marriages are traditional marriages in Pakistan. Arranged marriage is a type of marital union where the bride and groom are primarily selected by individuals other than the couple themselves, particularly by family members such as the parents. In some cultures, a professional matchmaker may be used to find a spouse for a young person.

In the U.S., while the divorce rate however around 40 or 50 percent, the divorce rate for arranged marriages is 4 percent. In India, where some estimate that 90 percent of marriages are arranged, the divorce rate is only 1 percent. Are low divorce rates a sign that arranged marriages work?

An arranged marriage is a marriage arranged by someone other than the persons getting married, curtailing, or avoiding the process of courtship. The term "arranged marriage" also applies if parents do not have a direct involvement in selecting the spouse.

In Pakistan in the 80's and still now there are arrange marriages. One of the church members brought a family to our home. They proposed to my parents and then they asked us to meet at friend's home see if it is okay. My mother asked me if I have anyone else in mind, I said no. In those days' guys feared coming close to me and my sister as my brothers were considered very strong, they all were six feet tall I have four brothers so had no boyfriends of likes. My father-in-law was sick, so he wanted his son to get married soon. This family came to our home on 18 November 1980 and then my father-in-law became ill and died on 20th of December 1980. That is how I got engaged and married and moved to America. My husband's sister, who was a doctor, sponsored us to come to US.

Interesting thing is if it a arrange marriage the family pays for the wedding etc. My four brothers helped pay for the wedding with my parents. My youngest brother was paid the most. There were 800 invited guest but due to one of my middle brother being the karate champion and the famous playback singer being in the wedding party 400 came uninvited in those days they did not count the guest or looked at the RSVP they thought if we asked the guest it would be family's insult the food was shortened my brothers have to buy more food. I am not sure how they managed it, but I know it was a seven-course meal served first time in my town. My Muslim friend said it is lady Di's wedding she got married at the same time.

After living in US for 42 years when I look back how the weddings were arranged, I can just laugh at it. My mother picked up my maid of honor and asked me we want to have her friend's daughter my maid of honor as her engagement is broken and her mother came to me that she will be busy with the bride so she will not go into depression. This girl was from the same school as I did but not close to me, I wanted my best friend to be my bride's maid however I couldn't refuse the logic of my mother at that time. Now sometimes I think about it, and I regret it since I never had any contact with my friend after the wedding and once, I went to Pakistan I heard she passed away.

Arrange marriages in my opinion are not good for girl's morale since you do not know who you are going to live with, if the two are compatible and or if their past has scars or so which can influence the relationship, also there is no respect, however in Pakistani and Indian culture the arrange marriages last long due to the family bindings. There is a reason that the arrange marriages are considered to last long since all the family members are trying both parties to stay together no matter what. In my lifetime I have seen women are abused by their spouses and the rest of the family members and there is no way out, once you are married no matter how hard the problems are you must not quit your marriage. They stay in this unhappy situation till the day they die. I understand bible tells you one marriage, arrange marriages are mentioned 17 times in the Bible.

"Many of the marriages mentioned in the Bible were arranged marriages in which the parents were involved in choosing a mate for their children. The practice of arranged marriage varied greatly from one family and one community to another. However, many cultures have practiced arranged marriages from the earliest times. For example, Abraham commanded his servant to find a wife for his son, Isaac (Genesis 24). The servant found a potential wife for Isaac, Rebekah, but Rebekah was given some choice regarding whether she accepted the offer (verses 57-58).

In summary, arranged marriages were standard in ancient times, and the Old Testament contains several examples. The practice of arranged marriage arose from a strong sense of family and fidelity that often helped provide a stronger commitment to the marriage covenant. However, many marriages in the Bible were based on a formal arrangement in which both the man and the woman desired to be married."

Another common criticism of arranged marriages goes something like this: arranged marriages are not built upon informed desire. Since partners lack familiarity with each other, they cannot be expected to possess any genuine feelings for each other. ... Arranged marriages work in the same way.

Yes, arranged marriage! ... Since it is your parents and extended family that has decided on the marriage, you will never even think of doing anything that would make them feel embarrassed. There is, therefore, a lot more respect between the two people than there is in love marriage.

Parents arrange child marriages to ensure their child's financial security and reinforce social ties. They believe it offers protection and reduces the daughter's economic burden on the family due to how costly it is to feed, clothe and (optionally) educate a girl.

Advantages:

1. Arranged marriage is generally accepted in our society as it lends creditability and social recognition for a secured conjugal life. The entire responsibility of the marriage is undertaken by both the parents.

2. In Laws adjustment is better in case of an arranged marriage.

- Disadvantages of Arranged Marriages
- Love is often not a factor.
- There may be no fit at all between partners.
- Potential higher divorce rates.
- Separation may be difficult.
- Spouses may not trust each other.
- People may be quite unhappy.
- Family problems.
- No room for personal choices.

The early days of my marriage were very difficult to live with the new family. We stayed after the wedding in my father in laws soap factory somehow there were bedrooms and bathrooms, and kitchen was built in that factory. Still remember the second day of my marriage my mother-in-law came in my bedroom and said you are married, and I became a widower. I did not understand what she meant by this her husband died in December they arranged this marriage after two months what is my fault? I stayed with the mother in laws for three months or, so it was very difficult some days. I went hungry to teach no one cooked food in the morning in that household, when I reached school one of my cousin sons, who is my nephews Gulbaz will bring paratha and egg for me to eat in the lunch break. One day I was so sick I remember my mother-in-law told the servant not to go upstairs only Garcia [full of ticks] their dog sat next to me till Albert came home. Each family member use to ridicule me only oldest brother-in-law Eric was nice with me. Things were very different in those days you cannot talk back it is against the culture. It is a typical mother-in-law story. I heard my mother-in-law accusing swearing at her sons all the time which was very new from my home. I never heard my mother swear or say any bad names to us. One day the dog Garcia died my mother-in-law buried him in the factory she advised us not to tell anyone since it was rural area and there was new bride in the house so no someone can come steel the jewelry or clothes etc. One night I heard someone walking on the second floor near the bedroom area we packed our clothes and went to stay with my parents until we moved to US.

CHAPTER III
Moving to USA

---

a. Relationships with in-laws and sponsoring family

We moved legally to United States my sister-in-law who came to US in the 60's, she was the doctor (Neonatal) and sponsored us. We will always be grateful to her for her this action of kindness.

We moved to USA and stayed in Boston. When we came I had only $400 in my pocket, and we stayed for couple of weeks with my sister in laws home in, Massachusetts, and other sister in laws home also in, Massachusetts.

Relationship with in-laws, sponsoring family was intense. It was very difficult to live and look for a job there was no guidance. Sometime my sister-in-law living in Somerville, will ask me to leave the house since she was studying for her PhD program. I will wonder in the streets of downtown Cambridge and central square. We stayed with family for a month or so every weekend we will go the older sister and weekdays we stayed with another sister-in-law. The older sister-in-law did not want me to cook at her house she will give us two toasts and will say people do not eat in the afternoon in America, when we come back from work, I will make food. The younger sister-in-law will tell me to cook the food for the entire week and serve ourselves whenever we need food but stay outside the home so she can study. Sometimes she will lock the house I did not know where to go I will walk in the streets and pass the entire day walking in Central Square. It was harder to live with either of them, but it was a learning experience I made me strong.

b. Hardships getting job, going to school with small children.

I had the teaching background in the early 80's was preposition 2 1/2 on public education 1980-1984. We did not apply for any teaching jobs. My in laws did not help me to find a job however, on the contrary they found me a volunteer position in Hospital in Bacti lab. While doing the volunteer job at a Hospital I did not know what volunteer work I was too young or naive, it was work with no money. One day I saw an ad on the bulletin board there is rooming house nearby and room is available. I went to see the house and the owner was a lady she was very nice to me, and we moved to the rooming house the landlady. She treated me very well I made her pan cakes in the morning she will ask me to give her the breakfast. She was an angle and guided me to get an apartment in the Malden area. The neighbors were also very nice in fact my in laws did not invite me for our first thanksgiving in US the neighbor invited me to come to their home and have dinner with them.

In the early 80's jobs were scarce. I got my first job it was a seasonal job at the Jewelry store "Longs Jewelers" in downtown as a salesclerk. I do have to mention here that one of the in law guided me how to interview if you need a retail or any job in US. It was helpful when my sister in laws husband who was a doctor, explained me how to interview for a jewelry shop however, he himself is a well-known Neurologist.

We lived a very simple life not spending too much and saving. Albert worked in Anthony's Pier 4 Restaurant, as a bus boy and it was very hard to get into teaching those days were hard it was preposition 21/2 in Massachusetts education system, he also did not even try to look for a job in teaching field per what was communicated to us. My first job was a seasonal job on summer street in Boston at Longs Jewelers, I was very happy that I have a job. It lasted few weeks and then I worked on the assembly line at a factory near my home in Malden. Riveting for the radio factory in after the summer lay off. I got a job in the bank as a teller the bank sent me to school for ATM were introduced new way of banking. I got the A in the class was very happy of my achievement. We used to go to NHD a hardware store, after dinner at home that was our entertainment, after work and saved our money. Life was simple I stitched my own dress and skirts to save money, we bought a singer sewing machine from a yard sale it was very useful. We did not eat meat as it was expensive eggs were, 69 cents for a dozen will boil eggs and make potato and egg curie and rice for dinner. We saved so much money on little jobs we were doing.

Our first vacation was in Montreal it was our honeymoon. My husband had gone to school at McGill University he knew the area and people around Saint Catherine Street so wanted to show me his friends and the school. We rented an apartment for ten days and had fun visited many places will go out to eat. When we came back our brother-in-Law asked us how much money you spent over there, we told him little bit more than seven hundred he was amazed that we spent so much money on our honeymoon. At that time $700 was a lot of money.

Montreal was a very beautiful and clean city it was nice waling on the cobble stones and watching the different shows in the evening. We met many people from my husband's school life at McGill University.

Visiting Montreal in 1981

We had our first child a beautiful daughter Sarah in the early 80's, we were very happy at her birth that we conquered the world. Albert, while driving the car and will hold baby in his hand. She brought us a lot of joy to us we did not know how small of a house we were living in; how little we have. We will invite many people, from church our friends and neighbors in that one-bedroom townhouse in Malden, Mass. My sister-in-law will always condemn that why we have so many people in our home. We moved again to another house on Townsend Street in Malden this apartment was in a house the third-floor apartment was next to congressman Ed Markeys's parents' home. At that time, I was not much interested into the American Politics. After couple of years we moved to Everett, Massachusetts in a bigger apartment still working in a bank and then we got our American citizen ship and at time we decided to sponsor all my siblings who lived in Pakistan. The main reason was so that they and their children have a better life in US.

I got a job at PK 5 digital credit union for ATM bank teller position it was in Maynard Mass. The life was still very hard Albert worked at night and I worked in the morning. I will drive from Everett Mass, and he will be coming from Watertown mass and transfer the baby to him early in the morning in Arlington at the arranged road site area. At that time there were no cell phones I am not sure how we did this; God was taking care of us we never missed work. Then he will take the baby home and I will go to work. At the credit union one of girl advised me to buy a condo in Leominster it is a nice city we drove and looked at the condos. She told me it was a growing city the prices were reasonable it was in the middle of 1984.

We bought a condo in Leominster. I was still working in the banking industry. My father came to US without even calling or letting me know that he will be coming. I got a call from one of Pastor in New York hello your dad is with us we are bringing him to your place. My father was visiting Pastor Mahboob Khan, he never told me that he was coming. So, it was surprise in 1985. So, my father stayed with me in our condo. I was filling papers for my siblings and their families we took my father when we filed the sponsor ship in Boston since he was with us, I never gave thought that he will stay in US. One day my mother called and said can you keep your father in US. Sure, we had our first child we both were working we thought it will be good idea to file his papers as well. He took care of my daughter while I was working.

I was on family way; I must quit my job at the banking industry since I couldn't drive that far. I worked for US Census for few months while I was pregnant my boss Judy Smith, was nice and she gave me the job in those days it was not easy to get a job while you are pregnant. I had the second child; the child was a second blessing to us we were very happy. After the baby I got a temporary job in a Plastic company through an agency for three months. My mother-in-law stayed with us one day I came back from work, and she told me to take the girls and get out of the house. I drove to the nearby hotel stayed in "Day's inn" called my brother he advised me this is US this is your home why did you come out of the house I told him we have been taught to respect our elders we cannot say anything back to the mother-in-law. Anyway, I called my older sister-in-law [Dr. Ophelia Mall] she was nice with me and told me to go back to home she will ask her other brother to bring her to his house to I went back to my home the next day.

While working at Gary Chemicals, I saw one young man coming after college and working in the company, I asked him to bring me the college brochure he was telling me all good about the University of Lowell Plastics Engineering. Albert worked in the same company at night, and he advised me to pursue my schooling and told me that I the brain I can do it. I went to open house with my three-month-old baby in my lap the professors were very nice and talked to me friendly way and guided me what subjects will be good for me. I got the admission in the fall semester prior to going to school we took a short trip to Karachi to meet the family in December 1989.

After coming back from the trip, I went University of Lowell and got my master's degree in Plastics Engineering. We moved to Lovell university student Lowell housing. The teachers were very nice and help full they supported me. My advisor was 89 years old professor and other professors of plastic engineering encouraged me. I used to stay in the library till the librarian kick me out at the midnight I studied very hard. One of my professors told me just work and study like a mad woman then you will succeed I just followed his advice some semesters I took twenty-four credits and I received all "A". I am so thankful to my Lord gave me strength to move forward. I always remembered this verse Exodus 15: 2. The Lord is my strength and song, and he is become my salvation: he is my God, and I will prepare him a habitation; my father's God, and I will exalt him.

I am always thankful to my parents whom I called Aba and Ami they use to drive from Leominster to Lowell to baby sit my children and cooked food for us. Albert worked hard since there was one income, he did two jobs one his regular work and delivered pizza in the evening. I sponsored my mother as well since I was going to school and had no one to support while they were staying with me. During this time, I sponsored my parents so they can enjoy the freedom of United States.

After I finished my degree program in 1992. We moved back to Leominster in our condo. While I was still working on my thesis and searching for a job, we had a fire in our building in May 1992 and we moved out to the condo Red Cross put us in one room hotel nearby at the hotel. In the same hotel the next morning. I saw in the newspaper a local company is looking for someone with Plastic knowledge to join them. I was in my jeans since there was a fire in our condo, we left our belongings there I did not have my resume I went and asked after reading the add, the fire chief if he can let me in just to get my resume, he went with me, and I took my papers and went to the interview. It was a miracle I got the job God helped in all the way. God is an awesome God; he has helped me in all the steps of my life. We know our Lord helps us in the worst time of your life. Psalm 119:147 I prevented the dawning of the morning and cried: I hoped in thy word.

There were only two days allowed to stay in the motel we have to move out and stayed, red cross asked us if we know anyone, we can move the condo will take x number of days to be fixed. We stayed with my father. Again, we were to look for an apartment since we cannot move back to our condo. I was looking for the apartment at the same time while looking for job. I saw the first add in the newspaper someone was renting a townhouse. I went to see the Landlord and told my story how my Condo was damaged with the fire and no place to go; this Landlord was a God sent angle he did not ask me any question or reference he gave me the keys and we got the townhouse. I did not have to give him the deposit. Again, this was a miracle for us no reference no deposit for a decent size town house, Psalm 46:1-3 God is our refuge and strength, a very present help in trouble. Therefore, will not we fear, though the earth, be, removed, and though the mountains be carried into the midst of the sea. Though the waters thereof roar and be troubled, though the mountains shake with the swelling thereof. Selah.

People were very nice and helpful we moved into this apartment. The story of condo was that we did not want to move back as the we found out the fire was suspicious so to not the pay the mortgage one of our friends advised us to declare chapter 11 in this way you will get rid of this condo, we declared bankruptcy. If some would have suggested me now, we would have never done that however we were too naive at time did not do what to do. We stayed in the town house for a while, and I was reading the newspaper and saw an ad that the builder can build you your house if you are working. With too many questions in our minds that our application will not be accepted since we just declared the bankruptcy, we went to see the builder in Leominster and told him our situation that we will not be able to get a loan from the bank. The builders said just fill out the application and they reviewed our application and said no problem we will build you a house, we will help you get the mortgage approve. I believe that God has helped me in mysterious ways. We stayed in that townhouse until we built our home in 1994 in Leominster mass this was our eleventh move in US but thank God it was in one state only. All praise goes the Him who is the mighty and helped me all the way of my life.

Gitto Global job I published a paper in the plastics journal on recycling of polyurethane foam which, this was based on my Masters of Plastics, thesis I presented this paper at the annual ANTEC conference was published in the annual technical conference of plastics engineering preceding.

I worked in different Plastic Companies as their Product Development Manager or Director. until 9/11 hit my job was gone since the plastic company, I was working could not supply forks to airline industry and they decided to let me go. I was out of the work for almost nine months that is the longest I had ever been out of work.

Bringing Siblings to the great country USA.

As mentioned earlier, when I became citizen of USA, we decided to sponsor my siblings to US so they and their children can enjoy the life of USA. We filed petition for my three brothers and one sister in the category relative sponsorship visa. It took thirteen years for them to come to US. I had to file the petition again in 1998 now there were 24 people because I had to file to support for their spouses and their children my husband supported me for this issue. All together there were twenty-four people. They arrived in 1998 and stayed with us in our home in a four-bedroom, we had a large basement and a large living room somehow, they managed to sleep on the first floor one of the brothers with his wife and two boys will go to sleep at my parents' home and their one son will stay back. Then they will come back the next morning and have stayed all day in our home. I advised them to come to one family at a time and then once they are settled then another family may come but it was not the case. Three families came just a week apart that year 1998 was a very different experience in our lives my children are born in US there was communication issues with the new Pakistani cousins there was a cultural shock to all children. It was a lifetime experience. Same time I lost my job at Gitto Global where I was the product development manager, I was laid off at the same week when the families arrived in Massachusetts to live here. Maybe it was God's plan. Sometime God works in mysterious ways. I am sure it was a blessing for me or my extended family, since I have to bring truckloads of food every day, we had 24 people to feed. I arranged their housing and jobs. While my siblings were in Pakistan, I asked them to come one family at a time so once one is settled then the next family can come but I guess they were very anxious to come to USA and seems like they were competing so three families came a week apart, however God gave us strength and energy to manage. I took my brothers and brother-in-law to local plastic companies to have assembly job and sister to the grocery store so they can start working and one by one we moved them to their rental apartments. My older brother came at the last with his family and stayed with us for six months since he was an electrical engineer but couldn't get a job in his field.

We always thought we will treat our new immigrant families as we were treated. With food and sometime took them out to seashore for picnics etc. We tried our utmost best to keep them happy in this way some time I have to admit that doing that sometimes, I had ignored my own children also. We were thankful that God had provided us.

Sometime when you bring families from other country you bring their problems with you. My youngest brother had family issues and he will run back to Pakistan. We were in the process of buying a store somehow, he convinced us to buy a rental property he brought cash from Pakistan there was no credit history so the realtor refused to give him the house so he asked me to buy the house and he will pay the rent and establish a credit history once he has the credit built up, he will buy the house from me. It was a triple décor house in Fitchburg I bought the house and with that house came the problems. The tenant did not pay the rents and so did my brother. His family moved and my younger brother left them with me and went to Pakistan again. His family stayed in the house few months later we had issues with the tenants, and we hired a rental realtor who tried to help collect the rent but was not successful and every month we came to know that it is tenants' rights more than the landlords in Massachusetts. We sent the notice to all the tenants to vacant the place we want to sell the property. We wanted to do it quickly so we can get a store. My brother sent me the rent money after long talk, he was okay for his family to move it took almost six to nine months to vacant the building. While it was on market my two brothers in Fitchburg apartments and my older brother's son were so scared of the bugs in the house. I decided to give them this building so they can move in with my equity they did not have to pay any down payment as I transferred my own equity to them and even, I paid for their first mortgage. The banker was so surprised he said I have never seen a sister helping like this giving a property to his siblings without any cash they do have to take over the mortgage the property was for $42k. I advised them to pay half and half mortgage and get over with this loan from the bank.

c. Discrimination in workplace and daily life, travel

We bought a small breakfast place Fitchburg, Mass. We were so happy we converted the breakfast place into a grocery store we called the store Sitara Market, India Pakistan groceries store.

The store was not in a good location however we were trying to run it but 9/11 changed our idea of this store when people started looting the store and three times store was robbed one time they tied albert with ropes and a doctor who was doing shopping at that time was tied up when the robbers ran away and someone came in and untied their ropes the doctor said I had a knife in my pocket I am a surgeon why I did not think about the using it. It happened so fast no one can think what to do. Some time we will get a call from the police someone is vandalizing your store please come. Our church folks will come in the daytime to stand with us and supported us.

The store was looted by the robbers several times due to our looks from Pakistan local people considered us terrorists, our church people use to come and sit in the store to guard the store for couple of months. The last attach was on my husband and a doctor who was shopping in the store and thief tied them with the rope and looted the store that was the turning point we closed the store. This was the first time I felt we are treated as second class citizen in the great country of USA.

We decided to shut the store gave all the groceries to the food pantry at our church.

Racism is a typical prejudice of human race. It varies from person to person and culture to culture, but it is common to all nations. Racial discrimination is one of the typical sociocultural practices in American society. Racial discrimination is a based-on ethnicity, language, skin color religion etc.

After 9/11 all my thinking got changed about the great country of USA. I had two major incidences in my personal life one was the small accident I was driving my Mercedes to go the store in Fitchburg and the driver came from the right side in front of my car and clipped my car with his car he was driving a PT cruiser. The police came in he knew the other driver and gave me the citation although I explained him how this guy game from my right side. The police officer did not listen to me and was laughing and talking to the PT cruiser guy. Never this happened to me, I felt like this citation was given to me because I was not blonde and white.

The second incident was that after I lost my job due to 9/11 at a plastic company, I was the director of engineering at Aaron Industries we lost many businesses due to not selling folks and knives to the airline industry, I could not get the job. We did not know why since my degree was in great demand my church friends looked at my resume, I was writing my two undergraduate degrees from Pakistan. One with Chemistry and Biology major. This was the second time I felt I am not from this world it is a prosecution. Well, I had the same experience in Pakistan was not new to me. This was when I got exhausted for looking for a job after a year. One of the reasons was that there was one Pakistani, Muslim woman was "Aafia Siddiqui" for helping al Qaeda, she studied at MIT. Aafia was also called "Lady al-Qaeda". The last news I read was that Aafia Siddiqui a Pakistani neuroscientist with degrees from MIT and Brandies University who was convicted on multiple felonies, she is serving an 86 –year sentence at the Federal Medical Center, Carswell in Fort Worth, Texas [19]. Some of my friend read about this woman in the newspaper or news and told me this is the reason why you cannot find a job. My friends from church helped me modify my resume and I asked my pastor Rev. Hoyt for special prayer he prayed with me church letter that I am a member of Methodist Church of Leominster and asked me to send this letter with my resume. Prayer and that letter from church were effective that week I got three job interviews and offers. I believe in prayers it does help some time it takes a little bit of time. I got a very good job in elite medical device company.

This medical device company hired me as Scientist for plastics here again I had to face discrimination I had a woman who had an issue against my accent she said derogatory remarks about my ethnicity and my accent, I must report to the manager, and she was removed. During this time, I was fascinated with the sterilization process, and I published a paper on the E- Beam Sterilization I have to special permission from the lawyers at Boston Scientific. The same paper I presented in the annual engineering conference for plastics engineering in Chicago, USA. I took both my children at the conference so they can learn from this conferenced. My manager advised me that you are a high energy person why do not to you pursue for further education BSC will pick up the cost of my schooling. I went UMass Lowell for PhD program. At the same time, I was working on the very high visible project to design the catheter to withstand e beam sterilization process. I was really interested in the neuroscience. I was always eager to learn how the brain works and specially the Alzheimer's disease which is a problem in our society. Here again our brother-in-law advised me to stay in the same field what you have been working in because people are doing research for several years it is not worth to deviate from your own field of Plastics Engineering.

The project involved a lot of time and energy I was going to school at night. I had to travel to Minneapolis as well as to Galway Ireland all the time for production trials. I also have, to attend the related subject matter conferences, which now I am proud of that I did that I attended the IRAD radiation world conference in Antalya, Turkey. However, I worked there for four years I was the in charge of the plastic lab later. I felt more racism when the organization made me in charge of the plastics lab. It is very difficult to work in a hostile environment. Every day when I drive to work, I use to read Psalm 54: 2-4, also while driving to work I will listen to famous CD, or Dr. Paul Dinakaran You are not alone. I will pray so the Holy Spirit will come over me and blanket around me after this prayer I felt safe to go this workplace. I had always this prayer in my heart

"Father, you have called me, and I have answered you. I do not know why you chose me, but I thank you. Help me to do my best to live up to the confidence you have placed in me. Amen."

There was no time to finish my schooling could not attend the entire classroom setting classes so both my advisors called me and advised it is not worth for you pursue this degree you are not in the class any way you are already in-charge of lab why do you need this degree we can give you Master of Science in Biotechnology. I took their advice and got another master's degree.my advisors advised me with all your work we can give you another master's degree in Biotechnology.

In 2005 I went to Methodist mission schools to study be a leader in the study program it was India and Pakistan studies. I was the study leader for this program. This Leadership program was to teach in different schools and universities about the word of God. This study was so interesting that I went into the depth of searching for the religion and Pakistan how it came to India and Pakistan. There was another lady Easter in the group when we read all the history and persecution, we said we will write about this. I did teach in Pennsylvania and Gordon College same year my mother passed, away in Leominster. I did not take very seriously when my mother passed away it hit me after next three months, I was sick and sad and went for therapy. I know I used to cry in the middle of the night the only little puppy knew I am sad. This was our little pet dog Rani. As it is said that dogs are the best friend of human, she has proved it.

Going to United Methodist Mission study program gave me incentive to think about and write how and why the Persecution going on in Pakistan. During this Leadership training program and teaching in different conference. Now with the social media and world has come so closer that you get the news in few seconds from all over the world.

My mother prior to passing away her wish was that all her children are in the USA she wanted to give up her home where we lived in Drigh Road Cantt, Karachi for the house of worship. My father made that house Dorothy house of worship. There are five congregation praying in this house. Let me tell you at this point there were no new churches allowed to be built in this country at that time since it is Islamic Republic of Islam.

[https://www.persecution.org/2020/07/04/islamic-seminary-declares-construction-new-places-worship-non-muslims-pakistan-unlawful]

---

d. Travels:

Most of my friends have asked me since I travel so much for job and fun to write something about my travels, however I have travelled many places in this section, I am writing a synopsis of my travels.

I am praying so I can travel to all those countries where Jesus disciples have gone for preaching so far, I have four countries where his disciples have gone and were persecuted as well.

Since we move to USA my first Travel was to USA was in1977.

My father was in Pakistan International Airline and my parents both travelled abroad every year in 1977. I accompanied them to the big USA we stayed with my brother in New Jersey and then were invited the Mission trip to Mississippi. This was lifetime experience Pastor Price who invited us to see his Church and be a part of the mission school studies for Methodist Ministries. We went around to Savanna Georgia there another Pastor took us to different churches to talk about Christian life in Pakistan. In this trip at one church all I remember people did not want to shake hand in 1977 due to racism. I did speak up in the church that Jesus Christ was from Middle East, and we worship our Lord and his son. To this day I did not know if people there liked me or not.

We also went to Chattanooga Tennessee my father had a rich friend who had carpet mills we stayed at his resort was lovely experience.

1993: Chicago:

I went to a medical device show in Chicago. During this show met Alan Shepard. Alan Bartlett Shepard Jr. was an American astronaut, naval aviator, test pilot, and businessman. In 1961, he became the second person and the first American to travel into space, and in 1971, he walked on the Moon. In those days we had polarized pictures.

Fig.4 Picture with Alan Shepard at the trade show in Chicago in 1995.

Travel to London 1995:

Trip to England we decided to take our children to England to meet show them the English culture we stayed there for three weeks. Friends arranged a musical program at brother (Aja's) home brother Asif played the tapla. We used to get up early in the morning and go to see the changing of the guard. We visited the madam Tussauds Museum, London bridge and botanical gardens.

Fig 5. My daughters and London Bridge in 1995

Turkey 2006 :

This was a lifetime experience staying in the resort Renaissance Antalya Beach Resort & Spa, s the place, a 90,000 square-meter (22-acre) pine-shaded paradise in Beldibi, 23 km (14 miles) southwest of the city of Antalya on the way to Kemer, Olimpos and Phaselis. I got to see where Sant Paul preached in the amphitheater and several thousand people came to hear him. This place was near the sea Mediterranean and Beldibi meets.

Fig. 6 Near the amphitheater where
Saint Paul preached in Turkey

My hobby is anthropology I always visited ancient churches wherever I have travelled. In Turkey I visited the amphitheater where St Paul use to preach.

This conference ended abruptly as there was shooting in Antalya and we have to catch the first plane to get out to the country. Interesting enough the first flight was going to Germany I took that that flight to Frankfurt and called my Uncle Dr. Inayat Gill in Cologne and stayed with his family for two days.

Colonge Klon Germany 2007.

There I visited the oldest church called Cathedral Church of Saint Peter) is a Catholic cathedral in Cologne. It is the seat of the Archbishop of Cologne and of the administration of the Archdiocese of Cologne. It is a renowned monument of German Catholicism and Gothic architecture and was declared a World Heritage Site in 1996. This church has been a religious site since 612, the present church was constructed between 1151-1257 it is one of the 12 great Romanesque churches of cologne. This was eye opening for me a very old church and there were so many tourists visiting this church.

[https://www.cologne-tourism.com/]

Fig. 7 Walking out of the Saint Peter Cathedral 2006

Ireland 2004

During my tenure at BSC I traveled a lot. My project resided in Ireland, so I went to Galway Ireland. As my hobby is anthropology went to the monastery. Galway is a Harbor city on Ireland's west coast, sits where the river Corrib meets the Atlantic Ocean.

2005 during the daytime I worked on the catheters and my project on a small-scale trial and in the evening, I will go to the nearby restaurant over there the sundown is 11.00 pm. There will be music in the small restaurant and people play guitar and violin. One thing I noticed that the folks were very nice in the small towns however their teeth are not great maybe they did not take care of their tooth like we do in America. Here I visited Saint Nicholas Church of Ireland parish, which covers Galway city. It was founded in 1320 and dedicated to Saint Nicholas of Myra, the patron saint of seafarers, in recognition of Galway's status as a port.

Another highlight from our jaunt along the east coast was Dunguaire Castle (pictured above and below), a 16th-century tower house on the southeastern shore of Galway Bay in County Galway. Bus trip to see Kylemore Abbey, County Galway, Ireland.

Europe:

In 2004 I decided to go to Europe tour with my younger daughter and my friend Kara Goeken who also worked with me at Boston Scientific. We went to Amsterdam, Holland, Germany, Poland, and Scotland. This trip was via train from Amsterdam to Germany and Poland. The most interesting part in Poland we found that we can get on big jar of bear for one dollar not me my nephew bought, and a hamburger was also one dollar. Groceries were very cheap.

Fig 8 The famous wall Brandenburg gate monument before the division of east and west Germany

We flew to Scotland and stayed with my cousin for couple of days my friend stayed in the hotel nearby. We stayed in Glasgow. Glasgow is a port city on the River Clyde in Scotland's. It's famed for its Victorian and art nouveau architecture. Famous for, textiles and engineering; most notably in the shipbuilding and marine engineering industry. It is a hub of Scottish Opera, Scottish Ballet and National Theatre of Scotland.

We went to Edinburgh and saw the famous Castle.

Fig. 9 Scotland Edinburg Castle 2004
Kara my friend, Sophi and myself

Edinburgh is Scotland's compact, hilly capital. We went to see the castle and it rained. Edinburg castle stands on the castle rock from iron age. Fair

Fig. 10 Edinburgh castle 2004 kings' row we did shopping.

India, Pakistan, and Dubai trip 2010

This long trip we took my nephew was getting married in Karachi Pakistan. Within the same journey I decided to go to India and Dubai as well in this way I do not have to take a separate trip.

In Karachi we stayed for three days for the wedding and hopped up in the airplane to go to Delhi India. My first cousins Zenobia's husband was a Bishop for church of CNI, so it made easy for us to travel within Punjab for four days he gave us a car and driver very convenient. There is a lot of poverty in India Delhi the young children will come in front of the car from nowhere when we stop the car at the traffic light or on the road to view the scenery.

We went Agra in the car. Halfway between Delhi and Agra lies Vrindavan, just ten kilometers from Mathura, the actual birthplace of the ancient Hindu deity, Lord Krishna, believed to be the eighth incarnation of Lord Vishnu. We stopped at Vrindavan since I was watching a drama series and as soon, I saw the name we asked the driver to stop we looked around all small temples are built in this town. I couldn't believe that we are there. It was real.

After stopping there for an hour, we drove to Agra our destination. We stood in line to buy taj mahal tickets. It is interesting we did not consider ourselves as foreigner since we were the same color and looks stood in line to buy the tickets with local people my cousin Zanobia told us since we came from Delhi just stand in line here. One of the lady officers came and told us we look foreigner so go pay 700 rupees instead of 20 Rupee. My cousin said you guys look local why are you charging them more money she said they do not look local. I was surprised since we were wearing the same shalwar kameez what other folks were wearing but I guess our style of standing stood out and they charged us.

I t was 105°F degree and people were walking in the bright sunlight no matter they were used to this heat. The Taj Mahal was built in 1648 by Shah Jahan as a memorial to his wife. Today, it is listed as one of the new Seven Wonders of the World. Mughal Emperor Shah Jahan lost his wife Mumtaz Mahal on June 17, 1631. Today, the Taj Mahal is listed as one of the New Seven Wonders of the World

Fig. 11. Sophi looks very tired after going through the customs near the entrance of Taj Mahal. I was not that impress as I have read and heard about its beauty it is made with white marble.

Taj Mahal has an interesting story. Mumtaz Mahal born on April 6, 1593, she was the daughter of Abdul Hasan Asaf Khan, a Persian nobleman and the niece of the Empress Nur Jahan. When she was 14, she was engaged to marry Prince Khurram, also known as Shah Jahan. They were married in 1612.

Mumtaz Mahal travelled with Shah Jahan and even accompanied him on his military campaigns. Shah Jahan trusted her and gave her his Imperial Seat. Mumtaz Mahal and Shah Jahan had 14 children. On June 17, 1631, while she was giving birth to their 14 child, she died. Her body was buried in a walled garden in Burhanpur, on the banks of the Tapti.

Shah Jahan was devastated by her death. He went into mourning that lasted a year. He had her body exhumed and taken back to Agra in a golden coffin, escorted by their son Shah Shuja. In Agra, her body was buried in a small building on the banks of the Yamuna.

Shah Jahan started planning a royal mausoleum for his wife. The construction of the mausoleum began in 1632 and was completed in 1648. This tomb is made of white marble and is a showpiece of Mughal architecture. It is supposed to represent Shah Jahan's vision of Mumtaz Mahal's home in paradise. The architecture of the Taj Mahal combines elements of Islamic, Indian, Persian, Ottoman and Turkish styles of art. The principal architect of the Taj Mahal was Ahmed Shah Lahauri and thousands of artisans and craftsmen were employed during the construction of this monument. The white marble was sourced from Makrana in Rajasthan, turquoise from Tibet, lapis lazuli from Afghanistan, jade and crystal from China and sapphire from Sri Lanka and Arabia.

That evening we came back to Punjab same day I think it was eight hours drive to Ludhiana. Punjab.

During our travels in India, we stopped by in McDonalds to compare the food with American burgers.

Fig. 12 Raja burger was spicy, but the French fries were very crispy -McDonald's in Delhi India

We also visited Golden Temple during our four days stay in India. This is called seventh wonder of India. We also visited the Golden Temple. Golden Temple is a gurdwara located in the city of Amritsar, Punjab, India. It is the preeminent spiritual site of Sikhism. The man-made pool on the site of the temple was completed by the fourth Sikh Guru, Guru Ram Das, in 1577. This place is gold plated and rich community of Sikh support this worship place. This was my third visit one was 1966 and then in 1980 and now in 2010.

Fig. 13 beautiful snap taken by me of the golden temple in 2010 We did go inside and saw young children praying and reading their religious book

Dubai, we stayed in Dubai for couple of days we visited the tallest building of the world Burj Khalifa the world's tallest building, but that day they did not let us inn due to the construction on the 25 floors. The Burj has highest number of stories in the world, 160 stories and 2,716.5 feet height. Then we went to Palm Island and Atlantis the first Palm Island made in the ocean it was breath taking. It is too bad I did not take the picture of Burj or we were looking for my sister in law who was in the shopping mall and were concerned about her health. On the other had she was enjoying her shopping in Dubai. As Dubai is a city and emirate in the United Arab Emirates known for luxury shopping,

Fig. 14 Atlantis Palm Island in Dubai 2010.

2011 San Francisco Bay Area:

I had to take a trip to see a client in San Francisco with the engineering team while working at Medtronic. This trip was amazing as after the meeting we went to San Francisco Bay area to walk on the board and the entire group went to the brewery.

Mexico 2012 work related trip:

Fig.15 entering in Mexico border from US

Fig 16. Walking through the boarders with the laptop in 105 ° F

Mexico Entrance I have to park my car in border near El paso Taxes and walk through the boarder at that time it was a $25 fee I paid to enter the city. It looked like I have entered some Pakistani city. The person who was told by the company I was visiting to get me from the boarder he told me that he cannot carry my laptop since the border police is very strict. I had to walk from one end to the other end of the boarder in 105 °F Temperature more over I was told that there will be shot guns in this area so be careful. I was visiting one of my clients in the city of Juárez. The most dangerous city in the world announced in 2010. I was not aware of the fact until, I came home and watched a movie that weekend of Denzel Washington, Man on Fire 2004 and heard the name of Juárez. The next day when I returned to work all my colleagues were asking me which part of Mexico were you when I told them they had told me I am nuts without even knowing you went to that city. After this incidence I always check where I am travelling too.

Sometime people think it is fun to travel and work. It does have its pros and cons to work related travels.

2012 Rome & England vacation.

In 2012 I wanted to see Rome and we travelled for two weeks in Rome. I took this vacation with my cousin sister-in-law. We used to get up early in the morning and walk around all day site seeing and then come back in the evening for rest. The interesting part was that at time we booked the trip with the travel agent for the hotel but the day we reached we found cheaper and better hotel in good location. The day we landed in Italy the cab driver told us that Pop Paul is going to have a prayer in an hour at Sant Peters square we went straight to Saint Peters square people told us buy any souvenirs from here and those will be blessed by Pope Benedict XVI. We bought several roseries and scarfs and stood in the line for the prayer.

Fig. 17 After the worship and prayer after
Pope Paul, saint Peters Square.

Saint Peter's Square is a large plaza located directly in front of St. Peter's Basilica in the Vatican City. This square is named after Saint Peter, both the square and the basilica are named after Saint Peter, an apostle of Jesus considered by Catholics to be the first Pope.

I loved the food in Rome everything tasted so fresh. Pizza with balls of mozzarella cheese was one best food there. You can eat so much without even gaining weight.

Fig. 18 We visited the colosseum is the most prominent
example of ancient Roman architecture. Here you can
be robbed by the photographers they wanted cash.

Fig.19 Sistine Chapel ceiling design I took this
picture without the flash as they do not allow
due to the preservation of the painting.

I took this picture Sistine chapel this is so amazing design however similar
paintings we saw in a church in Prague. The Sistine Chapel is a chapel in
the Apostolic Palace, in Vatican City and the official residence of the pope.

Rome is full of chapels with the google search I came to know there are
900 Chapels in the city of Rome Italy.

Fig.20 Pieta (1498–1499) is a work of Renaissance
sculpture by Michelangelo Buonarroti, housed
in St. Peter's Basilica, Vatican City.

Fig. 21 Saint Marcus Florence Italy.

We visited St Marcus Piazza also known as St Mark's Square, is the principal public square of Venice, Italy, where it is generally known just as la Piazza. Piazza San Marco its vertical dimension is the campanile, the tall brick bell tower for the basilica

Fig. 22 City of Venus is the city also called the canal city it has 100 small islands in a lagoon in the Adriatic Sea. It has no roads, just canals, including the Grand Canal thoroughfare which is lined with Renaissance and Gothic palaces.

Same Trip we stopped in London since my cousin has never visited London, we took journey break. We went to same old placed the London Bridge as we have learned the poem in the primary classes and eye of London. Few snaps are below

Fig. 23 Eye of London. The London Eye, or the Millennium Wheel, is a cantilevered observation wheel on the South Bank of the River Thames in London. It is Europe's tallest cantilevered observation wheel in 2011.

2012 Amazon Jungle Rain Forest Vacation & Ecuador:

This was an amazing vacation above all the vacation we had at that time. Albert was working as a teacher in the Riobamba University he said to bring children to see the University we decided the other route to go to have vacation in Amazon Rain Forest we searched on google and found a resort in Amazon near the Ecuador only. My older daughter accompanied me we met Albert in Quito the capital of Ecuador spend couple of days in Quito. Quito, Ecuador's capital, sits high in the Andean foothills at an altitude of 2,850m. When you drive in the city it seems like a fortress. We visited the oldest church in Quito, Basilica of the Nation Vow is a roman catholic church is the is the largest neo-Gothic Basilica in the Americas. It is a catholic church it was Sunday morning we worshipped in this church was impressed with the architecture of the church.

Fig.24 We worshiped in Basilica of the Nation. It is the largest neo-Gothic Basilica in the Americas.

Pope Leo XIII approved the construction in 1887, and the French architect Emilio Tarlier was brought in to design the church: inspired by the Notre Dame and Bourges cathedrals, began his designs in 1890, and finally, on July 10, 1892, the first stone was placed.

It took more than 30 years to build the basilica. The first mass and the first ringing of the bells took place only in 1924, Pope John Paul II blessed the church in 1985, and it was consecrated and finally inaugurated in 1988.

Fig.25 The front of the Basilica of the Nation

This picture was taken in front of the church it is the largest church in the Americas.

Fig.26 My daughter standing on the vicinity of the Basílica del Voto Nacional: the largest neo-Gothic church in the Americas.

We also went to the Monument & plaza marking the equator, which is known as the middle of the world very interesting to watch people taking pictures of this site. The grounds contain the Monument to the Equator, which highlights the exact location of the Equator and commemorates the eighteenth-century Franco-Spanish Geodesic Mission which fixed its approximate location. The weather in Quito is same year around people are not that tall they are slightly brown colored people were very pleasant during the entire trip.

Fig.27 in the middle of the world line. The equator runs through in Ecuador.

Some time I am frugal during the vacation since people know you that you're a traveler and charge more money. We decided to the bus tour in Quito by travelling in the local bus and sitting in the bus until it reached the last destination where the bus stops, we got down and walked around the local village and asked the driver when he will take us back after an hour the bus was ready, and we went back. This was our site seeing trip.

Fig.28 In Tena the tour of the rain forest included the
boating to cross the river amazon to the jungle.

We stayed in Tena 4 nights in nice huts which were covered with leaves
inside the hut was one bedroom and living area. Travel by bus into the
Amazon Jungle for five hours from Quito to Tena. My older brother called
us and told us not to go there as people can be killed during the bus ride
and no one can find you. You can also take a airplane but we prayed and
went via bus the bus was circling around the mountains and we can see the
deep ditches and old rack age. These might have fallen over the years and
no one bothered to help them out. At one stop two cops came in I think
we were crossing the boarders and searched every one, there was a older
lady in front of our seat they questioned her a lot and found stuff we do
not know what she was carrying she was knitting throughout the journey.
We arrived at the resort late afternoon. The distance from Tena to Quito
is 191 kilometers (119 miles) and it takes about 3.5 to 4 hours driving to
get there. Tena is a city in the Amazon rainforest of Ecuador. It is the seat
of Tena Canton, as well as the capital and largest city of Napo Province.

The next morning the guide took us to a local Quichua family in their
small village. We walked there and saw how the family is making beer from
the white radish. We also learned how they make the pottery dishes and
do the hand painting on those dishes. It was interesting culture.

The next day our tour guide took canoe ride and went across the amazon
river. Guided walk tour to a waterfall. Learnt about medicinal plants or

an afternoon jungle walk. There were many plants which we have seen in Pakistan and India however here in rain forest looked interesting.

Fig. 29 Indian dress up for village tour in Tena

Those four days went so fast my daughter did not want to come back to Quito she wanted to stay there. We said this is all we can do here and spend some time alone from the rest of the world. We must go back to reality.

This is the first time in our lives we stayed in the huts for vacation. The huts were regular rooms with attached bathrooms with screen window the screen was nets so bugs will not come into the rooms. The sounds of the birds, monkeys and amazon river flowing was so peaceful. No TV or any internet at that time. We just did not care for it this was the best vacation ever.

Fig. 30 inside the hut – Amazon Jungle

Fig.31 the entrance and front of the hut

The amazon Jungle Hut where we stayed outside, and the top was the hay stalk inside was regular room.

2014 Trip to Las Vegas

I was working in San Diego someone told me Las Vegas is very close from here. As being adventurous I called my friend Kara Geoken to come so we can explore this city in Nevada.

This is the 26th-most populous city in the United States, the most populous city in the state of Nevada, according to Wikipedia. It is also called Vegas, it is an internationally renowned major resort city, known primarily for its gambling, shopping, fine dining, entertainment.

It is interesting to note that throughout the stay at this resort and we did not spend a penny on the gambling. My friend and myself had very conservative ideology.

We visited my places here in Las Vagas enjoyed the food and learnt the history of the Mobs we went to see the Mob Museum: Explore a dark but fascinating side of Las Vegas at The Mob Museum in downtown Las Vegas. This modern museum, formerly an old federal courthouse and post office, provides a one-of-a-kind view of the history of the mob and the role it had in the creation and history of Las Vegas.

We were amazed to see beautiful statues in Las Vegas. After travelling in different state each state has its own beauty.

I am always amazed by the beautiful country has to offer. There are kindhearted people here when I mentioned to Kara that I am writing our visit to La Vegas she advised me to mention also how the doctors were helping the homeless folks on the street. I guess these doctors are the one who are called doctors without borders.

Fig. 32 This picture was taken after
we watched a bird show.

My friend Kara Goekin we worked together at Boston Scientific we are friends since 2003.

We also stpped by at Hoover Dam and read the history. Hoover Dam is a concrete arch-gravity dam in the Black Canyon of the Colorado River, on the border between the U.S. states of Nevada and Arizona. It was constructed between 1931 and 1936 during the Great Depression and was dedicated on September 30, 1935, by President Franklin D. Roosevelt.

We took a bus to see Grand Canyon from Las Vegas is Grand Canyon West Rim, which is 128 miles or approximately a two-and-a-half-hour drive from Las Vegas.

Entrance of the Grand Canyon West

I have heard a lot about Great Canyon and now we are there it is amazing how nature has made these marks on the land for thousands of years. Grand Canyon West is a census-designated place in Mohave County, Arizona, United States, located on the Hualapai Reservation. The population was two at the 2010 census. Grand Canyon West is home to the tribe's Grand Canyon business operations, including the Grand Canyon West Airport and the Grand Canyon

Fig. 33 This picture is taken by me at
the Grand Canyon. March 2014.

2014 Bahama Trip a pleasure trip

This was my first cruise water. After my younger daughter's wedding we decided to take a cruise however Albert couldn't join us due to his leg pain issues. We couldn't get the refund back since it was the last-minute issue. The ship was beautifully decorated inside and outside. All kinds of foods were available. It was fun trip.

Fig.34 Entering the ship - travel to Bahamas

Fig. 35 This was a beautiful picture I took when the ship was leaving the doc this is all Miami

Fig.36 Sarah and me enjoying the weather in Bahamas.

The site seeing was interesting but the sicky weather was unbearable.

Fig.37 These seashells were worth seeing and the
tour guide had a whole history behind these seashells
how he collected them how the snails come out.

Israel 2015

One Wednesday our bible study group went to Baptist church in Fitchburg there the preacher came from Jerusalem. Pastor Jimmy DeYoung was preaching in that church and announced. He asked that anyone who is interested in Jerusalem. I take groups to Jerusalem I always wanted to visit this country I signed up for this trip and went in March 2015 to Bible study group to Jerusalem organized by Jimmy DeYoung;s ministries. I went alone in this trip was for 12 days. We met in New York with other members of the group and flew Turkish airways. To landed in Tel Aviv there the tour bus organized the JD ministries picked us up and went to Jerusalem. As soon as we landed in Tel Aviv It felt so serene as Jesus was there when we reached. All tour groups were Baptist except my self being Methodist. We toured around Jerusalem in the morning we had a bible study and then during the day several bible studies when we reach any point of interest. The size of Israel is equal to New Jersey state.

The first day was the preaching on the Mount of Olive by Dr.Jimmy DeYoung's while he was preaching we saw the shepherds were coming back with their sheep's it was mind blowing scene. First day we went to see the house of parliament where 1947 Israel was created. Although this country was created after the World War II its history is 4000 years old

We visited Yad Vashem where the museum is built six million holocaust victims and their name is recited all day long. The candles are lit 24 hours in this museum, Jews are supporting this museum to keep the memory.

This is a Holy Land the three great religions live here and claim this is their land. This place is occupied by the Jews, Muslims, and the Christians. We went to visit the western wall which is occupied by the Jews at this place King Solomon had built the temple.

Fig. 38 Wailing wall several people including me inserted the prayer request in the gaps of the wall and then walk backwards. Several of my friends asked me to put their names on the papers as well.

The Wailing Wall or Western Wall, known in Islam as the Buraq Wall, is an ancient limestone wall in the Old City of Jerusalem. It is a relatively small segment of a far longer ancient retaining wall, known also in its entirety as the "Western Wall". The Western Wall, or "Wailing Wall", is the most religious site in the world for the Jewish people. Located in the Old City of Jerusalem, it is the western support wall of the Temple Mount. Thousands of people journey to the wall every year to visit and recite prayers.

Looking at the center where western wall is the Dome sits on the rock and then the church the temple of the. The Dome of the rock building s considered a shrine and not a mosque. Men pray instead at the Al Aqsa Mosque located 650 feet (200 m) to the south. Muslims believe that this is the place where Abraham nearly sacrificed his son Ishmael. The Dome of the Rock was erected by the Muslim ruler Abd el-Malik in 688–691. This area is heavily guarded by Muslims, and they do not allow tourists to hold hands or be close to the women. During this tour my friend Paige was taking the pictures with her mom and dad who were in the tour, and they all were putting their arms on each other's shoulder like a family picture the Muslim guard came and took their camera and destroyed their pictures and told them not to hug or come close in this scared place. We were very surprised of this action of the Muslim guard; throughout the tour we never felt this experience in any area it seemed like they were controlling the human movements in this area. We were not allowed to enter the Dome of the Rock. It was emotional experience at this place.

Fig. 39 The Dom and me within the
Muslim area in Jerusalem

We went to see the Dome and the Temple of the Dome, it has beautiful art and writing outside this however they do not allow us to enter.

I had a conversation with another two men on the Temple Mount and asked them if a Kafir (كافر – a term for a non-believer) is ever allowed in? They both said no. One said that non-Muslims had not been allowed in since the Second Intifada in 2002, which happened after then-Prime Minister Ariel Sharon visited the Temple Mount. The visit was seen as an incendiary action to many Muslims in Israel and the Palestinian territories and sparked violence. I'm not upset or offended that Muslims would choose to keep their holy sites from being a circus of tourism. At the same time, I detest the idea that historical artifacts are off-limits to those of the "wrong" faith, especially from visitors who come with respect and a desire to learn.

Fig.40 The church of Mary Magdalene
can be seen from mount olive

A overview of the temple form the mount olive Elevated higher than the Temple Mount itself, the Mount of Olives offers a breathtaking view of the City of God and provides a natural resting place to pause, pray the pilgrim's prayer of thanksgiving, and prepare for the final approach to the Temple courts across the Kidron Valley. The Church of Mary Magdalene (Arabic: كنيسة القديسة مريم المجدلية, Russian: Церковь Святой Марии Магдалины) is an Orthodox Christian church located on the Mount of Olives, directly across the Kidron Valley from the Temple Mount and near the Garden of Gethsemane in Jerusalem.

Fig. 41 This is a directional pillar to Bagdad, Jerusalem.

All Directions pointing toward Jerusalem.

Fig. 42 The beauty of Israel is that some places there are domes and no greenery and some places it is so green no one can tell there are domes.

Fig. 43 A view of temple from inside in Jerusalem

2015 Dominican Trip for work

I have gone to Dominican twice, but this trip brought some memories I had to visit an injection molding company, People were nice however the place was not safe as the hotel folks did not allow me to walk outside the hotel and watched my room was under surveillance. I was surprised why my employer let me go to this area. I saw only men in this area with cowboy boots and loaded guns even at the company I was visiting were guards with loaded guns. The company knew that I will not come back again.

Fig. 44 The famous Calle Las Damas
Street dedicated for women

In the evening after work my client took me to this area where women use to walk in the 1511 this street was dedicated for women. Las Damas was the first street of Santo Domingo, Dominican Republic, and America. Located in the Colonial City, it owes its name to the fact that at the beginning of the colony the ladies strolled along that street, which is currently decorated with colonial tiles.

Just on the walking distance from this colony city was house of columbas. It is the museum now. The Alcázar de Colón, or Columbus Alcazar is the first fortified Spanish palace built in the Americas.

Fig. 45 The hose of Columbus in Dominican

One of the most popular museums in the Colonial City is also its most impressive in architecture. Completed around 1512, this Gothic and Renaissance style palace was once the home of Diego Columbus, son of Christopher Columbus, and his wife María de Toledo, niece of King Ferdinand of Spain.

I visited Cathedral of Santa María. According to Wikipedia, the Cathedral of Santa María la Manor in the Colonial City of Santo Domingo is dedicated to St. Mary of the Incarnation. It is the first and oldest cathedral in the Americas, begun in 1514 and was completed in 1541.

2016 Trip to Trinidad, West Indies February for work

It was just a trip for two days but brought some memories of old country. I was so excited to see the old Indian culture here in this area of the world. Trinidad and Tobago is one of the wealthiest countries in the Caribbean, thanks to its large reserves of oil and gas, the exploitation of which dominates its economy. Trinidad's capital, Port of Spain. Trinidad is the larger and more populous of the two major islands of Trinidad and Tobago. The island lies 11 km (6.8 mi) off the northeastern coast o

Venezuela and sits on the continental shelf of South America. It is often referred to as the southernmost island in the West Indies. Why do I see more Indians here because after the British government abolished slavery in 1834, Asian Indian and Chinese laborers were brought to Trinidad as indentured servants?

When I asked the hotel receptionist what is here to see he said just a block away is famous Indian cricket player Kali Charen House. I walked outside see this modest home, when we were in Pakistan, we use to watch him on TV making sixers, brought some memories.

Fig. 46 The parliament house Trinidad was also in walking distance from my hotel.

2016 Cuba Mission Trip

During my visit to Holy Land, I overheard three pastors talking about the Cuba trip. These pastors were the part of Holy Land trip in our team they were studying eschatology and were deeply interested in the bible preaching and learning. They told me the name of the pastor White in South Carolina brings people to missionary trips to Cuba. This was a very different trip in March 2016. The application included us to write our three generation from parental and maternal side. We have to buy reading glasses, jewelry and candy for the children so one suitcase was full of the all the goodies we brought for Cuban people. There was a charted airplane from Miami to Habana. The flight was short but expensive. We met our group folks at the airport 12 folks with five preachers were part of this group. It was interesting I have to work in Florida, and I carried my work computer and work phone as well they advised us to carry limited number of electronic as at the airport someone take away that. I worried during this flight that what if someone can grab my work computer what will I tell my company. Anyway, when we landed at Habana we must sit in the plane for several hours as the government did not allow as to enter the airport. At 2 am we were allowed to enter in the airport somehow, they airport folks knew Pastor White as he had a distinguished personality tall and gray hair. The lady at the counter did not ask any questions and let us go without even checking our luggage. I have to use the rest room; the airport rest room was the filthiest rest room ever seen in my travels. No flush and stuff were all over the floor. I have to get out and hold till the group went into a Van 14-seater and another Cuban pastor welcomed us and we went to our rooms. It was interesting when the morning pastor White will inform us that we will be travelling in three groups each group will go at certain location.

After breakfast the calls comes in and redirect our area to another location. As our travels were watched by the government. We had four Cuban ladies who prepared the breakfast for us every morning they will give us fried eggs, fired meet and salad bread and coffee/tea. We always had a translator who can translate what we have to say to the street people. It was a street ministry we will stop people and tell them about the cube called EVANGECUBE. It is a evangelism tool to spread the gospel. This one was "Simply Sharing Jesus". People were integrated by this cube and will listen to us while we share the word of God. Unfolding the answer of Life's greatest puzzle. There were six cube pictures we will show:

1. Show 'Man in Sin" separated from 'God".
2. Open to Christ on the cross
3. Open the tomb
4. Open to "Risen Christ"

5.   Open to "Cross Bridge"
6.   Open to "Heaven & Hell".

After displaying all the cube section, we asked the question "Would you like to trust Jesus right now and be saved". If the question was yes, then we would invite the folks to the evening worship service at some one's home. We also distributed reading glasses and the candy people were very happy and mostly all of them we spoke in the mornings will come back to worship service in the evening.

We were really impressed how people can live on $24 salary in a moth and will eat one meal and live in the government provided housing we also saw lines for ration. The super store or market had a few items of food and in very less quantity. Children were mal nourished where not healthy mostly babies were sick and the parents will come and ask us to pray for the sick children. Un healthy life stye they were issue with the water cleanliness. The house we were staying it was a military home with 6 bedrooms and three bathrooms. We saw there was another missionary group bringing in the clean water ministry in the area.

We all are fascinated about Cuba our younger generation want to have the nationalize system or socialist government. It was eye opening for me when in Cuba the officials sent us the notice that four people within the group of twelve will be tested for zika virus. The screening will be performed in the hospital. Zika virus was an epidemic at that time. A fever was developed which was caused by Zika virus, began in Brazil and affected other countries in Americas from April 2015 to November 2016. The World Health Organization (WHO) declared the end of epidemic in November 2016.

A doctor came to our resident and took us in the car when we reached there in that clinic I saw food was lying down in lab. The area did no seem clean to me so asked Pastor White that I do not like this area I don't want them to take my blood in this unclean environment however he said we cannot refuse it this point they will kick us out of the country I will go first and see If I die. Anyway, when the technician opens the glass testing slides and told us it is sterilized my eyes were opened since the wrapper was turned yellow the glass slide had lost its sterility, I again told pastor white these glasses are not sterilized or seems like expired the sterility period. Any way we ended up taking the blood test. The doctor asked me what I do for work how do I told him I work in medical devices and had worked on catheters to withstand ebeam, gamma sterilization processes. He wanted me to work with him on catheters there in Cuba the people there were using plastics bottles as catheters. I did not accept his offer as I was there for missionary work.

During the trip I asked pastor white I do not see the poverty here as everyone is dressed up nicely that evening, we went to the place for worship and saw how people live in a shack next to a nice home.

Fig. 47 The shack next to beautiful house in Cuba

A Shack can be built next to a nice home in cuba. Housing has been and is one of the main social problems of Cuba; some of its difficulties were inherited, others occurred during the Revolution.

We were amazed how people have kept their cars from 1960's these cars were when American boarders were open. Now here in US these cars are considered classic cars.

Fig.48 Panoramic view of Havana and
you can see Florida across

A panorama of Havana in March 2016 view of Florida from Cuba. One of the first things you notice as you enter Havana is the colorful vintage cars that line the streets. The classic car is as much of a Cuba. The story of classic cars in Cuba is full of political and historical significance. Cuba never had any car manufacturing plants. The 1959 Cuban Revolution and the beginning of the Cold War saw a change in the island's automotive industry. Fidel Castro placed an embargo on the US and foreign imports, which meant that no American cars were exported to the island.

Fig. 49 Havana cars used as taxi's

These cars are used as taxi in Cuba, and I wonder how they have maintained these cars in excellent condition since we did not have any business with Cuba after 1960.

Cuba still has old style telephone system. You can drop in the coins and talk or ask the help of an operator.

Fig.50 Visiting Earnest Hemingway this is the monument right in the city center.

Fig. 51 Hometown of Earnest Hemingway 'Finca
Vigia '. Albert taking a walk around the house.

Visiting the Ernest Hemingway, the famous American Writer who lived
half of his life in Cuba. monuments and the famous "Donavan bar ". The
monument in the town of Finca Vigia 1898-1961.

Fig. 52 Our mission group picture with Pastor White.

In Cubin flats owned by the government. Mostly folks live in these
apartments. This is a picture of places where we went to spread the gospel.
The hosing of Cubin folks how in a socialist countries people live. The
socialist housing, however, the positive aspect is if you paid the rent for
twenty some years you have 80% of ownership.

Fig. 53 The Christ of Havana sculpture

The Christ of Havana (Spanish: Cristo de La Habana) is a large sculpture representing Jesus of Nazareth, on a hilltop overlooking the bay in Havana, Cuba. It is the work of the Cuban sculptor Jilma Madera, who won the commission for it in 1953. This statue is 20 meters tall. 17 meters for the Christ figure and three meters for the base. This is the largest Christ statue in Cuba.

When we were in Cuba google just came to town and open its doors. Interesting we have to go at special park to post our stuff on the Facebook or call our children. This park was few blocks away from the place where we were staying.

2016 Amsterdam and Copenhagen

We visited Amsterdam in 2005 we were invited for a wedding of my cousin Gulbaz, daughter. Whenever we plan to that far we would like to visit the nearby places or countries as well. After attending the first ritual Mehdi of the wedding we flew to Copenhagen to explore the country of Denmark. Copenhagen, Denmark's capital, sits on the coastal islands of Zealand and Amager. This is also called the happiest city of the world due to cities fairy tales. Tivoli Gardens and for once being home to the children's writer, Hans C Andersen. Tivoli gardens amusement park was opened in 1843. The idea of the Disney world is based on this park. It was Halloween and my older daughter is a big fan of Halloween we enjoyed the hot vine and drinks in that cold evening.

Fig. 54 Copenhagen 2016 Tivoli gardens

Back to Holland

We took a day trip to the Vakantiepark Giethoorn is a canal city with beautiful homes along the side folks do have their own boats and bring their groceries and stuff in the boats. The quaint village Giethoorn in Overijssel is sometimes called 'Venice of the North'. In this village you will mostly find waterways; the ideal place for water enthusiasts! Giethoorn is part of National Park Weerribben-Wieden and consists of authentic farms, kilometres of canals and dozens of bridges.

Fig.55 This amusement park is worth seeing it is a tourist attraction
we rented a car and drove to this site it rained that day we still
enjoyed looking at the homes built next to water ways.

Fig.56 enjoyed the boat ride

Fig. 57 it was cold and misty afternoon and
Rura James was with us from Germany

J2017 visit to Utah

In Jan 2017. I was attending the sterilization seminar for work to get the certification and more information of the processes. While I was there, I visited the Mormon temple they did not allow me to enter the temple since I was not Mormon. The Salt Lake Temple is the centerpiece of the 10-acre, Temple Square in Salt Lake City, Utah.

Temple square

The golden angel statue is the symbol of Jesus Christ second coming. This temple is oriented towards Jerusalem. The Mormonism is a religion invented by Joseph Smith Jr. He wrote in his book that angle Moroni has visited him and presented the golden plates.

There are several religions or prophets who have come after Jesus Christ. As Christian we believe that Jesus Christ was the Last Messenger from the God and he will be coming back to take us to Heaven.

Fig. 58 In this picture captured the Steeple
with golden Angel Moroni statue

The Salt Lake Temple is a temple of The Church of Jesus Christ of Latter-day Saints on Temple Square in Salt Lake City, Utah, United States. It is the largest temple of the Latter-day Saints in the world. It was built in 1846 it took 40 years to build this temple.

2018 Spain and Prague November

As I said in the beginning it is my desire to visit each country where Jesus disciples have gone after His departure to spread the gospel. My goal is visiting these places where the disciples did their ministry.

Spain was considered the second safest country in the world in 2019. Spain, a country on Europe's Iberian Peninsula, the capital of Spain is Madrid. We planned to go to Barcelona as it is famous for its major Mediterranean port and commercial center and is famed for its individuality, cultural interest, and physical beauty. This city is about 90 miles from the French borders and one time known as the Paris of Spain.

Barcelona is a major cultural, economic, and financial center in southwestern Europe, as well as the main biotech hub in Spain. My daughter and myself planned to explore this city and then go to Prague for couple of days. As we know that most famous place to visit is the Ramblas, or Las Ramblas, is one of the most famous and iconic boulevards of Barcelona. Stretching for approximately 1.2km from the Port Vell to Placa Catalunya, this street is hugely popular with both locals and travelers alike and provides one of the main thoroughfares of the city. We came several time on this street while staying in Barcelona. We loved Barcelona for its stunning architecture, and world-class cuisine. As my daughter is vegan, we ate the best vegan food here in Barcelona. We visited several places most of the architecture was done by the famous Antoni Gaudí i Cornet. Below are some of the snap shots I took while we were there.

This picture was taken when we were left in the trolly to Montserrat . The Montserrat mountain and its monastery is an important symbol of Catalonia's history, spiritual beliefs and culture, and is also the home of the religious figure of the Mare de Déu de Montserrat, the patron saint of Catalonia. It is breath taking view from when you are in the left or walking towards the Montserrat. We read that in 1025 the Abbot of Ripoli and Bishop of Vic, Oliba, officially founded the Monastery of Montserrat. During the twelfth and thirteenth centuries, a Romanesque church was built in Montserrat containing a carving of the image of the Mother of God. Over this period pilgrims began to come to Montserrat.

Fig. 59 This picture is taken while walking
and viewing below in Mostserrat

Fig.60 the mountains and the statue in Mostserrat

In this place we went to see black Madonna. The Black Madonna was believed to have been carved in Jerusalem at the beginning of the religion. It is a wooden sculpture. It is one of the most famous Black Madonna statues in the world, and in 1844 Pope Leo XIII declared the Virgin of Montserrat the patroness of Catalonia. The famous statue is place very high and the there are several steps to take to see this sculpture. I was not that much impressed with this structure I thought it was over promoted.

Fig. 61 In front of the church in Barcelona

Fig. 62 LaSagrada Familia

We visited Casa Milia probably second famous building of Guadi architecture after LaSagrada Familia

Fig. 63 This was the gothic church in Prague called Church of Our Lady before Týn. The interesting part was it is 80m high and has been the main church of this part of the city since the 14th century.

Fig. 64 I took this picture in Prague one of the ancient churches, St George Basilica. This picture reminded me of Sistine Chapel in Rome. This church is no longer a church it is a museum. St. George's Basilica is the oldest surviving church building within Prague Castle, Prague, Czech Republic. The basilica was founded by Vratislaus I of Bohemia in 920. It is dedicated to Saint George.

We also visited the church of the Church of Our Lady Victorious, located in Lesser Town at the foot of Petřín Hill in Prague, doubles as a museum hosting what could be described as a permanent fashion exhibition for a statue of the Infant Jesus. Here the In the church where the original is housed, it is ritually cared for, cleaned and dressed by the Carmelite sisters of the church, who change the Infant Jesus. I was just curious how the dress was changed and donated by the followers. We also visited Inside of the church of our Lady Victorious.

2019 Montana

America is the most beautiful country in the world. I travelled for work to Montana it has its own beauty. The Treasure State is known for its abundant natural and mineral resources, including coal, copper, gold, manganese, sapphire, silver, lead, oil and zinc. This state is one of the beautiful states of America.

Fig.65 Perfect picture taken the cows
are grazing in Montana.

2020 England

We went to England for our friend's daughter's wedding and took some days to explore Bath and stone henge, In the end of Jan 2020 at time we discovered travelling to Stonehenge there were several Chinese travelling in the buses with the face mask on, my children advised me to wear the face mask it was the eruption of covid-19. At that point of time, we did not realize that US will be hit by this virus.

Fig. 66 The Stonehenge an me in England
prior to convid_19 in 2020

STONEHENGE is one of the biggest archaeological mysteries in the world – this prehistoric monument has been baffling researchers since Middle Ages. The landmark consists of a ring of standing stones that measure around 13 feet high and seven feet wide and weigh roughly 25 tons each. Experts believe that the monument, which was first excavated in the 1620s, was erected between 3000 and 2000 BC. It is not clear when and how it was discovered there are no written records found by the prehistoric culture this is the reason why these became the mysteries of the world.

We visited the Turkish bath in bath in England. In this trip I was accompanied by Adi and Sophi.

Fig. 67 Turkish Bath in Bath England

2021 Covid Limited travels so just travelled within the country. South Dakota

During the election of 2020 South Dakota was in news every day so we decided to visit this state. Being conservative it was interesting to visit a site which has become more famous. It was worth seeing this monument. The museum showed the history how this monument was built on the mountain and craftsman was amazing. During this vacation we also visited couple of national parks and the wetlands.

Fig. 68 the presidents and us - Visit to Mount Rushmore National Memorial Park

South Dakota is a U.S. state in the North Central region of the United States. It is also part of the Great Plains. South Dakota is named after the Lakota and Dakota Sioux Native American tribes. It has been discovered that humans lived here 500 AD. When you see the Badland National Park, it has 244,000 acres of land. Wildlife abounds the park can be seen while hiking and travelling, we saw mountain goats in our drive.

Fig. 69 Badland with the foggy look
in the back of this photo.

I did not include my all travels in this chapters only the travels which meant something to me.

2022 March

Vacation with our first grandchild.

The more recent travel March 2022, I did was in West Palm Beach in Florida the oldest church we visited was the church of The Church of Bethesda-By-The Sea it has beautiful stained-glass windows and Garden beautiful columbarium and outdoor courtyard, aside from the beautiful church, itself. reminds me of Gethsemane Garden of Israel.

Fig.70 The Church of Bethesda-By-
The Sea after the church service

The strange thing about this church was that the glass-stained windows are inside the church on the top ceiling. This is beautiful episcopalian church. This is the only church in these days those folks were well dressed no one was wearing shots or slipper well-dressed people reminded me the old times when we use to church or dressed up it was considered the special dressing day to worship our Lord, I kept the same practice now as well.

e. Maintaining relationship with God

All these years I have maintained a good relationship with my Lord who has given us this breath and Life. By walking on the footsteps of Jesus our savior.

I have learned in forty plus years living the Great country USA. That there will never be a relationship in our life that is more important than the one we have with God in Christ. We could say that we're a friend of the president or prime minister of your country, or perhaps even the heads of all states, yet nothing compares to being the friend of the Creator of the universe.

My parents gave their home in Karachi Pakistan for the Gods house of worship. My mother said if all our children are here in US and Pakistan does not allow to build new church, we can offer our home for worship. My father spent his last days maintaining the house of worship where he will go every year from Leominster to Drigh Road, Karachi Pakistan to see how the activities are going in there were five congregations came to worship in my parents' home.

Our relationship with God is more important than any other relationship that you'll ever have in your entire life. Here are some reasons why:

1. Our relationship with God determines where we will spend the whole of eternity.

Having a relationship with God, or not having it, clearly says where we will spend all of eternity after death. I learned that this relationship can only begin by repenting of our sin and turning to Christ for salvation. It simply follows that having a real, genuine relationship with God means that we have done that and are saved (see John 3).

2. **Our relationship with God powers us up for daily living.**

Our friendships and other relationships will drain us, but our relationship with God will power us up so that we can live a full life daily. When we give more importance to other relationships, you give away all that you have, including your time, attention, energy, and resources. When we prioritize our relationship with God, you receive more than we can ever give to Him.

The effects of relationships are even more visible when one is in the wrong relationships: "Bad company corrupts good morals" (see 1 Corinthians 15:33).

Having good friends influence us towards the good. Having bad friend influence us towards the bad. Having godly friends influence you t be godly, but having God as our Father, our friend and our everything transforms us into Christ's likeness.

3.   Our relationship with God will last for all of eternity.

Everything we have in this earth will fade away, be it riches, friendships, connections with big people, and even ourselves. Yet, one thing that will not fade away is God Himself (see Matthew 24:35).

Because of this, we should choose to invest ourselves in Him. Christ said, "Wherever your treasure is, there the desires of your heart will also be" (see Matthew 6:21). If we invest ourselves in worldly relationships, we will only reap worldly benefits. If we invest in God who is in and for all eternity, we will reap eternal harvests.

I believe in the power of prayer. As human some time we do think why God is not listening to us. However, at the end you will receive the answer to the prayers. Prayer also energizes the heart of a believer through the power of the Spirit. Consistent prayer also releases the power of God's blessing on your life and circumstances. Jesus said, "When you pray, go into your room, close the door and pray to your Father, who is unseen.

Philippians 4:6-7 do not be anxious about anything, but in everything by prayer and supplication with thanksgiving let your requests be made known to God. ... Therefore, confess your sins to one another and pray for one another, that you may be healed. The prayer of a righteous person has great power as it is working.

Matthew 18:20 (NIV) For where two or three gathers together as my followers, I am there among them." Ephesians 3:12 (NIV) Because of Christ and our faith in him, we can now come boldly and confidently into God's presence. ... When we pray together as a group, we are essentially asking God to show up.

Powers are answered I did pray for my both daughters to have good husbands for this I have asked Pastor Paul Dinakaran to pray, and he predicted at the end of 2014 my daughter will be married.

CHAPTER IV
Finding life's mission and purpose:

Sometimes it can feel like you don't have a purpose in life or like there's no meaning to what we do. You may be surprised to hear otherwise. We should not spend all our lives wondering life wondering if there is more to life than our daily tasks. Learn what it is like to live a life full of meaning and purpose.

Ultimately, we are trying to improve our life and live with meaning by finding our purpose. We want more zest, more flavor, more fullness. In the strictest sense, we want to become a better person. We want to wake up in the morning excited, jumping out of bed with a thirst for life that you have not felt since you were a child.

One of the greatest fears imaginable is the fear of being alone. That is because we were designed for relationships. In fact, we were ultimately designed for a relationship with our Creator.

But contrary to what we expect, it's rarely an obvious or straightforward path. The way is hidden by insidious forces, and the first step is to recognize them.

Jeremiah 33:3 New International Version

3 'Call to me and I will answer you and tell you great and unsearchable things you do not know.'

Rick Warren, founding pastor of Saddleback Church in Lake Forest, California, one of America's largest and best-known churches, shows you how to lead a Purpose-Driven Life. This Miniature Edition™ will help you understand why you are alive and God's amazing plan for you--both here and now, and for eternity.

I believe everyone and I truly believe that every single person has a purpose in life.

---

a. Becoming Matriarch of family, relationship changed with siblings.

When I established myself here in US my life purpose was to raise an educated family. My Lord helped me raise two daughters with graduate degrees from the best schools and universities in Massachusetts.

I became the Matriarch of the family by bringing and guiding the families from the old country and all Praise goes to our Lord who has helped me all the way to this day. One thing I must mention here the relationship changed with the brothers and sisters afterward. I have evaluated as written earlier it might be due to sibling rivalry or by each person's expectations if the expectations are not met the relationship, is changes.

Lesson learned that we need to choose to prioritize your relationship with God more than any other relationship you have, or you will ever have. He is worth all the pursuit. In fact, He's the one pursuing us. The following verses strengthen our relationship with Lord then humans.

Hebrews 12:2;NIV

Looking unto Jesus the author and finisher of our faith, who for the joy that was set before him endured the cross, despising the shame, and is set down at the right hand of the throne of God.

Beside the near family, God has given me a vision to have relationship with the extended family. Whenever I am travelling for work or pleasure, I will visit the family who lives nearby each time. God is great and Jesus is wonderful.

Family Reunion:

In 2007 I joined with my first cousin and held a family reunion in Washington DC. We both choose this state as it was the capital of USA. This reunion was at the thanksgiving weekend. There were 80 members of Bhatti family joined together with their children and grandchildren and very close family friends. My first cousins came as far as from Pakistan, England, and Canada. We planned first day; I presented the family tree since most of the new generation was not familiar with the family history. I started from the grandfather to the youngest Bhatti in the group. The next day was the musical program my cousin Asif Bhatti who is a Gospel singer played music and sang songs. Third day we arranged a party for my daughter Sophia for her high school graduation and Nathan Bhatti for his high school graduation, these were the memorable days, folks still remember how great the occasion was.

Fig 71. Bhatti Reunion - Family reunion fist pictures are adult and bottom picture includes all the children attending the reunion.

Jeremiah 31:3

The Lord hath appeared of old unto me, saying, Yea, I have loved thee with an everlasting love: therefore, with lovingkindness have I drawn thee.

b. "in God's eyes, there is no race, color, or creed.

In 2020 with the covid_19 spread there were also several riots on race and color.

Racism and issues dealing with race have been around since the dawn of man. Stemming back to the days before Christ, there are many Bible verses about race and racisms found in both the New and Old Testaments.

Although many people — even those who identify as Christians — may not know how to address race and racism as it manifests itself in the world's current climate, the Bible offers many comforting and direct verses that will help with repair, reflection, and healing. And although these are not substitutions for properly educating oneself on current events and ways to enact change, they can serve as a reminder of God's love for all people, regardless of gender, color, and more.

Other Member of the family:

Some of the cultures do not like dogs. In our household as I mentioned earlier, we had a pet dog rani she was the happiest creature of the universe, I think God has given us this dog as a therapy dog as she was with me on passing away of my parents. This dog was a birthday gift to Sarah from her father but when she left for college it became my baby. The first time I saw rani I said to Albert why did you bring this rodent in our home, but she was the part of our family the 15 years she was with us but during covid she passed away. We always miss us she has given us the unconditional love.

Fig. 72 me and rani

We visited the ARC Encounter a replica of Noah ARC built in 2016 was built in nearly in six years whereas Noah' Arc was built in 70 to 100 years. Modern Craftsmanship. This visit was in September 23, 2022. Another adventure trip to see the how God works in peoples lives and they come up with an idea of making the ARC.

Fig 73 – ARC Encounter in Kentucky

Witness:

I have always prayed to God, and he heard my prayers, especially when I pray fasting, during the covid 19. I made two requests to my Lord in October of 2020.

1. My job had lot of travelling involved so I prayed to God help find me a remote job
2. I prayed to my Lord so my daughter can conceive a child and I can become a grandma.

God heard my prayer I got the job in the same month and my daughter become pregnant Covid_19 did bring us good tidings.

My granddaughter Selena was born in July 2021. She is our first grandchild.

I need to mention here that I have asked all my Christian friends to pray for my daughter so she can have a child. One of my beloved Pastor Hakyoung Cho Kim told me if you pray passionately God hear that prayer. This is interesting to know that it really works.

I designed my home so the large room with higher ceiling is our prayer room where we have prayers often invite my non-Christian friends as well.

At present I am working as a principal consultant in the Medical Devices arena and for church activities I have chosen the path of my mother I am the president of United Method Women. We are serving the local community.

I will end this story with the following beautiful verse.

Psalm 27:13-14 NIV -

remain confident of this: I will see the goodness of the LORD in the land of the living. Wait for the LORD; be strong and take heart and wait for.

Bible guides in on the topic of racism:

1 Samuel 16:7 [NIV]

"But the LORD said to Samuel, "Do not consider his appearance or his height, for I have rejected him. The LORD does not look at the things people look at."

The Good News: Despite how you look at one another, God will always see you for what's inside your heart.

Exodus 22:21 [NIV]

"Do not mistreat or oppress a foreigner, for you were foreigners in Egypt. "Do not take advantage of the widow or the fatherless. If you do and they."

The Good News: You all were foreigners at some point. You have to love one another as if you are all the same.

John 12:34 [NIV]

"Do not mistreat or oppress a foreigner, for you were foreigners in Egypt. "Do not take advantage of the widow or the fatherless. If you do and they."

The Good News: God loves you no matter what. You should do the same to those around you. This is one of the most convincing verses in the bible for me Here Christ is not saying that love just Christians or Muslims or Jews He is saying Love one another.

Romans 10:12[NIV]

"For there is no difference between Jew and Gentile--the same Lord is Lord of all and richly blesses all who call on him"

The Good News: God loves everyone equally. It does not matter the color of your skin or how you identify. Here again it is emphasized there is no difference between the religion Lord is the Lord of all nations.

The Good News: The same way that God loves you, He encourages you to love your neighbors the same. Everyone deserves the same type of love; regardless of what they look like.

REFERENCES CITES

1 https://www.islamicity.org/11485/how-islam-spread-in-india/
2 [Pakistan Journal of Social Sciences Vol. 32, No.2] (2012), pp. 437-443] (2)
3 https://artsandculture.google.com/entity/pakistan/m05sb1?hl=en
4 https://www.worldometers.info › population-by-country
5 https://www.census.gov/popclock/world/pk
6 https://docplayer.net/175959830-Sermon-outline-what-does-the-bible-say-about-persecution.html
7 https://www.standingforfreedom.com/2022/07/yes-christians-are-being-persecuted-in-america-heres-how-we-can-respond/
8 https://dbpedia.org/page/Pakistan_Penal_Code
9 https://www.bbc.com/news/world-asia-48204815
10 Islam and Women's right overcoming Inequality by Azam Kamguian June 20, 2018 [https://centerforinquiry.org/blog/islam-and-womens-rights/] Reviewed the following sites to get information:
11 https://www.persecution.org/2021/02/19/pakistani-christians-endure-38-incidents-persecution-last-six-months-2020/?fbclid=IwAR371W7zDSV_Vgm_NPVWVkcbDhi9Bf2_IV_o1r9abwL9kSMC9Rgi_jRWHrE
12 Pakistan Penal Code (Act XLV of 1860)
13 Center for Reproductive Rights: _Supplementary Information on Pakistan, scheduled for review by the Committee on the Rights of the Child during its 72nd session, 2016_, (accessed March 2018)
14 http://www.fides.org/en/news/69678-ASIA_PAKISTAN_Another_Christian_student_kidnapped_The_number_of_cases_is_increasing_in_Punjab

MY PUBLICATIONS

All publications were for technical purpose for the Medical Device Industry and Plastics Engineering audience.

- "Determining the Biocompatibility of Nanomaterial's" 26 July 2009 Convergent Technologies. Devicelink.com/mddi. pharmalive.com- author Orpha James with Dr. Peter Bradly.
- "Evaluation of the In Vitro Biocompatibility of Various Thermoplastics with Nanomaterial's" December 2006. Thesis research for MS Biotechnology degree, author Orpha James
- "Electron Beam Compatible Polymers" paper presented and published at the ANTEC, 62nd Annual Technical Conference of Society of Plastics Engineers, May 16-20, 2004, Volume 111-Special Area 2004. Author Orpha James
- "Color, Colorants & Color Measurements," in Plastics Formulating & Compounding Magazine, issue of May/June 1996.Vol. 2 No.3. Author Orpha James
- "Recycling of Thermoset Flexible Polyurethane Foams into Solid Polyurethane Rubber," paper presented at ANTEC; Annual Technical Conference of Society of Plastics Engineers held from April 27, May 2, 1997 published in the Conference Proceedings Volume 111-Special Area 1997. Author Orpha James

DEDICATION

- I am dedicating this book in honor of my father whom we called "Aba" Mr. S. R. Bhatty and my mother whom we called "AMI' Dorothy Bhatty who has worked very hard to raise six kids.

- I am also dedicating this book to my beloved, payala bachca, my little grandchild called "Choti" Selena Belle. The precious gift from God to us. Thankful for His blessings.

ACKNOWLEDGMENT

I want to thank the following people who gave me an incentive to write.
Sam Naimat- Austin Texas
Carolyn Abbot- Westminster, Massachusetts
Pastor Hakyoung Cho Kim[Late] – Concord, Massachusetts
Gulbaz Fazal – Amersfort -Holland
Watson Gill- Holland
Saleem Bhatti- Covina, California
Kara Goekin- Dudley, Massachusetts
Asif Bhatti- England
Zenobia Mal – India
Dawood Bhatti [Late] – Gujranwala – Pakistan
Susan Strobel- Leominster – Massachusetts
Pastor Paul Biswas – Bangladesh (Massachusetts)
Pastor Frank Mall - California

My Family
Sarah James- Stoneham, Massachusetts
Sophia James – Marlboro, Massachusetts
Aditya Khedekar – Marlboro, Massachusetts
Albert James – Millbury, Massachusetts
Zubaid Chris Bhatty – Worcester Massachusetts

NOTES FROM THE FAMILY

Orpha has a unique and dynamic personality

God Almighty has given her a special forceful, gift of achieving whatever she sets her sight on in life.

After her successful life in studies having two masters' in engineering degree, she is now venturing in writing a book about her experiences in life.

I deeply admire and respect Orpha's personality the drive she has to get to her goals in life

- Albert James [husband]

My mother has been an inspiration to me all of my life. She has shown bravery and courage in the face of adversity and challenges and has always remained steadfast in her convictions. Her incredible sense of faith has fueled her moral compass and served as a guiding light. She has always been strong enough to stand her ground when all others around her tried their best to wear her down. I am proud of her for making the decision to share her story with the world.

Sarah James [daughter]

My mother has dedicated her life to helping others and she always shows up. When other needed her. She carries the torch of strong women before her, my grandmother and great grandmother carried this torch- my daughter Selena will continue to carry it along.

Sophia James -Khedekar [daughter]

My mother-in-law Orpha is a beacon of hope to everyone she meets. Her steadfast determination is second to none, and her resume as well as her family life is certainly a testament to that. She was a woman in STEM before Women in STEM was a thing. From working entry-level jobs as a newcomer to this country to reaching the top of her field, there is nothing she can't accomplish.

She has raised two wonderful daughters and has been a mentor to me. As a matriarch, she is fiercely protective and equally kind to her family. She gives unconditionally, which makes her one-of-a-kind. Hearing the stories that made her the woman she is today was fascinating and will certainly make for a great read!

Aditya Khedekar [Son in Law]

Recall of vivid memories.

I am Zubaid Chris Bhatty being the youngest brother of six, count my sister Orpha being the closest sister of all siblings. And I am personally grateful to her for all support and attention given to all siblings by bringing us to the USA besides of her unending educational and professional path.

We all remember her closeness to our parents and always a step ahead to help in everyone's life. I could not fathom at the times how my sister and I could in any way be similar, due to the difference in our personalities, but sure we look like big eyes like our mother.

She is always a vital member of our family.

Zubaid Chris Bhatty [Brother]

APPENDIX A

Pakistani Recipes [booklet] written [2001] when we owned a grocery store in Mass.

Introduction

This booklet is dedicated to my grandmother Bani Willow Ram.

I am writing this book for both of my daughters Sarah & Sophia who are born in Massachusetts and are not interested in Cooking.

I want to thank my mother Dorothy in guiding me in some simple recipes. Also, my sisters-in-law's Dr. Ophelia Mall & Parveen Bhatty [Late] who are excellent cooks. My sister Rebecca who has a B.Sc. in Home Economics advises me frequently.

In the last I want to thank my brother Obaid who is the only male in our family, who knows how to cook and enjoys it too.

Orpha James

This booklet is a combination of old and new recopies. For busy people like myself who have no time for cooking, but still want homemade food.

Helpful Hints:

- Always thaw meat into the refrigerator or microwave.
- Refrigerate meat while it's marinating. Bacteria from the raw meat may contaminate the marinate if kept outside.
- To refrigerate large quantities of leftovers, divide into small containers first. This allows the food to cool fast and keeps bacterial from multiplying.
- Shell from eggs will come out easily if pinch of salt or baking soda is added while boiling eggs.
- After boiling eggs put in cold water right away it will prevent black around the yolk.
- Mash potatoes while still hot. This will prevent potatoes from sticking.
- To Clean fish thoroughly and to remove odor from it make a batter of a little gram flour water and a little turmeric powder and apply on the fish. Set aside for half an hour, then wash nicely and cook it.
- Roast chicken or turkey will have pleasing brown color if you sprinkle a pinch of sugar over it before roasting.
- While frying oil on a metal pan a few drops of oil will help food non-stick.
- Always fry chicken and fish with I /2 tsp of oil to eliminate the odor before cooking.
- To prevent discoloration of fruits such as apples, bananas, pears etc. apply juice of lemon.
- To get strong aroma from saffron, always soak it in either hot water or milk for IO minutes.
- To skim at from soup quickly, dip lettuce leaf in soup. Lettuce picks up fat. Or if time permits, keep soup into the refrigerator Chill, skim off fat.

- To prevent biryani masala from sticking to the cooking pot cover the bottom of the pot with leftover nan or bread and then spread the masala on top of it.
- Vegetable like Cilantro, Lettuce, spinach will remain fresh for a longer time, if kept in paper bags instead of plastic bags.

Index

Spicy Tomato Soup

Tomato Rasam

Main Dishes

Chickpea Pilaf

Biryani Bombay Style

Kharai Ghosht

Meat Pilaf

Bombay Nan Chap

Tandoori Chicken

Egg & Potato Bhujia

Fried Cabbage

Besan Curry

Spinach & Potato

Egg Plant (Bangon Bartha)

Fried Okra (Bindi)

Omelet

Roti

Fish in Garlic Sauce

Salmon Steak

Desserts

Sheer Korma

Mango Ice Cream

Banana Trifle

Yellow Sweet Rice

Gulab Jamun

Ras Malai

APPETIZERS

Shammi Kebab

lb. nonfat minced meat (beef)
¼ cup chana dal, washed
3 garlic cloves
1/4 inch of ginger
½ pepper 3-4 cloves
I inch cinnamon stick
2 large cardamom seeds one egg, beaten
½ cup oil
pinch of salt
2 hot green peppers

Boil all the ingredients, except the egg. When it is boiled, and the water is evaporated, grind the mixture in a food processor. Form the mixture into balls and press to flatten so they are round patties. Grease a non-stick pan and brush egg on each of the flattened patties before frying. Fry on both sides until light brown.

Serve with garden salad, if desired.

Chick Pea Chaat

¼ tsp. Salt
2 cans of chickpeas
3 boiled potatoes sliced
2 fresh tomatoes, finely chopped one large onion, chopped
¼ pack of Tamarind (imly) microwave or boil until dissolved, separate seeds, if any
2 hot green peppers
I large lime
fresh coriander leaves

Add all ingredients together in a bowl. Add Tangerine water. Squeeze the Lime into the mixture. Then add the fresh coriander leaves.

Pakora

2 cups gram flour (basin)
½ tsp. salt
½ tsp. red chili
¼ tsp. baking powder
I tbsp. whole coriander seeds
3 tomatoes, sliced
2 potatoes, chopped
I large onion, chopped tsp. Anardana
I cup water
4 cups of oil (for frying)

Mix gram flour and all the ingredients with water, except the oil, until it forms a thick paste. Heat oil in a pan. When heated, add the mixture with a small spoon one at a time to make at least IO pakoras at a time. Cook until brown. Use sifter to remove from the pan. Repeat until all the pakoras are done.

Serve with tea.

Note: Use caution when frying. Oil is very hot.

Samosa

A) *Shell*
I pound *of* all purpose flour
2 cups *of* water pinch of salt
tsp of cumin seeds tsp oil

B) *Veggie Mix* Boil potato and peas Add cumin
Pinch of salt
3 green (or red) chili peppers
I bunch of Cilantro leaves washed cut.

C)
4 cups of oil for deep frying

Mix all A ingredients and knead the flour dough until well done. Then make small balls out *of* the dough and flatten them with a roller. Next, make squares of each of the flattened balls. Add the veggie-mix into the square then fold the square with one layer at the top into a triangle and press the edges so the veggie mix will not fall out. Deep fry the veggie triangles.

Meat mix can be substituted with veggie-mix

Baked Kebab

(Potato)

I lb. ground beef (boiled)
I lb. potato (boiled)
2 tsp. Chili powder
2 tsp. Coriander powder
2 tsp. Cumin seed powder one tsp. Papaya juice
I small onion, chopped
I Tsp. Gram flour
¼ tsp. salt
2 eggs

Mix all ingredients above, except egg. Set aside for one hour. Make rounded balls and flatted them to make patties. Brush the egg on each patty. Arrange in a I3x9 non-stick pan. Put in oven at 375°F for one hour. Serve with fresh garden salad.

CONDIMENTS

Mint Chutney

I bunch fresh mint leaves, washed, and separated from stem one large tomato
I small onion
2 gartic cloves
2 green chili peppers
I lime
1/4 tsp. Salt

Mix all ingredients in blender until puree form.

Tomato g Cilantro Chutney

2 large red tomatoes
I bunch of cilantro leaves, washed I small onion
2 garlic cloves
¼ ginger root
¼ tsp. Salt
3 green chili peppers lime

Mix all ingredients in a blender until puree form

DRESSINGS

Cucumber Riata

½ cucumber, grated Pinch of salt
Pinch of black pepper cup of yogurt

Mix all ingredients in a bowl. Serve with main dishes.

Onion Riata

1/4 cup finely chopped onions 1/4 tsp. Cumin seeds-zeera I-cup nonfat
yogurt
Pinch of salt
Pinch of black pepper

Mix all ingredients in a bowl. Serve with main dishes.

Loki/Dhodee Riata

1/2 lb. of boiled and grated Loki Pinch of salt
Pinch of black pepper cups of yogurt

Whip yogurt with a wire brush. Mix all ingredients in a bowl and
serve with a main dish.

SOUPS

Chicken Soup

8 cups water
¼ cup cooked chicken meat,
2 chopped onions
½ cups chicken broth
2 Chicken bouillons
¼ tsp. Grated lemon
I tbsp. Lime juice egg yolk (beaten)
½ tbsp. Butter
½ tbsp. Flour
½ tsp. Ajinomoto China salt & pepper
Grated cheese (optional)

Melt the butter and mix flour with it. Then add chicken broth slowly, making sure there are no lumps. Cook until smooth, then add lemon, lime, bouillons, chicken, salt, and pepper. When it boils, add Ajinomoto and reduce heat. Add beaten egg to the heated soup. Remove immediately. Serve in bowl. Add grated cheese, if desired.

Lentil Soup (Dal)

I cup Masoor Dal/ Urd Dal (washed)
6 cups water
I tsp. salt
½ tsp. Pepper
1-2 Green chili peppers
2 tbsp. oil
½ tsp. Zeera (Cumin seeds)
I garlic clove
I tomato
I onion, sliced
Pinch of turmeric powder

Combine dal, water, salt & pepper, chili peppers, I tbsp. oil, garlic, tomato, and turmeric powder. Cook for 40 minutes. When it becomes a yellow uniform mix, stir it. Heat oil with cumin seeds and onions. When it becomes brown, mix it in with the dal.

Oil can be substituted with butter. Serve hot.

Makes 4 servings.

Vegetable Soup

½ medium sized cabbage, shredded
2 Carrots, cut into strips one celery stalk
½ *pound* tomatoes, skinned and mashed
I piece of cauliflower broken into tiny flowerets one cup green peas
I potato, cut into pieces Meat stock or water salt Pepper
Small bunch of parsley
½ stick butter
½ gallon milk

Heat butter in a large saucepan and sauté the cut vegetables lightly. Add tomato, cauliflower, green peas, and water with a pinch of salt and pepper. Cook until the vegetables appear to be well done. Reduce to lower heat. Stir in the milk gradually. Add salt and pepper. Garnish with parsley and sprinkle cheese, if desired.

Spicy Tomato Soup

3 cups tomato juice one and ¼ tomato puree
3 tbsp. sugar
5 whole garlic cloves
a dash of ground cloves I onion, sliced
2 chicken bouillon cubes dissolved in 2 cups of salt water
2 bay leaf

To make tomato juice:

I pound tomatoes
¼ cup cream
I tbsp. whole spices
I tbsp. cornflower
I tbsp. butter salt
pepper lemon juice

Boil tomatoes and whole spices with 3-4 cups of water, until tender. Strain the juice, and then add the bouillon cubes. Stir in cornflower and fry lightly. Add tomato juice slowly, making sure there is no layer forum. Bring it to a boil, stirring consistently. Boil I minute.

Serve with crackers, if desired.

Tomato Rasam

4 large red tomatoes
I large onion
I tsp. Cumin seeds
½ tsp. Peppercorns
6 garlic cloves
I bunch of coriander leaves
4 red chilies
I tbsp. oil
¼ tsp. Mustard seeds pinch of fenugreek seeds Salt

Wash the tomatoes and boil with four cups of water until the tomatoes are soft. Mash the tomatoes after removing skin. Grind together the cumin seeds, peppercorns, and garlic coarsely and add to the tomato liquid. Slice onion and break chilies into small bits and add to tomato liquid. Heat the oil and fry the mustard seeds and fenugreek seeds. When seeds begin to crackle and tum lightly brown, pour into tomato mixture. If it is too thick, then add a little water and bring to a boil. Remove from heat. Add chopped coriander leaves to garnish.

Serve with rice.

MAIN DISHES

Chickpea Pilaf

2 cups Basmati Rice
½ tsp. Zeera (cumin seeds)
½ tsp. whole cloves
½ tsp. whole peppers 2-3 cardamom seeds
I ¼ cinnamon sticks Bay leaves
cup of oil
tsp. Salt onion
One can of chickpeas (can be substituted with green peas)

Fry chopped onion until golden brown. Then add cardamom pepper, clove, cinnamon and bay leaves. Fry until brown. Then add washed Basmati rice and stir in salt. Add 3 ¾ of water after approximately ten minutes. Drain chickpeas or green peas and add to rice. Cook at medium/low for 5 minutes. When all the water is evaporated, rice is done.

Serve with Riata (yogurt dressing).

Note: You can also add a couple of red potatoes cut into pieces in rice, if desire

Biryani Bombay Style Pilaf

I lb. Beef/Chicken/Mutton with bones
4 cups Basmati rice, washed
2 onions, finely sliced
3 medium tomatoes (or can of tomato puree) one tsp. Garlic paste
½ tsp. Ginger paste one cup plain yogurt
½ cup Shan masala-Bombay biryani
I cup oil

Fry onions in hot oil until golden brown. Add tomatoes and stir until the oil separates. Add garlic, ginger, potatoes, yogurt, and Shan biryani mix and meat. Fry for 15 minutes. Add 1-2 cups of water and cook at low heat until the meat is tender. In a separate pan, add 12 cups of hot water and boil the water. Add 1/2 tsp oil. Then add washed Basmati rice. Boil until half cooked. Remove from heat and thoroughly drain the water. Spread the cooked meat and curry over the rice in two layers. Cover the pot and cook on low heat until the rice is fully cooked and tender.

Serve with Riata.

Kharai Ghosht

2 lb. boneless meat
6 tbsp. oil
2 cans tomato puree
I tbsp. salt
I 1/2 tbsp. red chili pepper powder
½ tbsp. garam masala '/2 coriander powder
2 tbsp. curry powder
½ tbsp. ginger paste
½ tbsp. garlic paste
4 green jalapeno peppers bunch of coriander leaves

First, wash the meat. Heat oil in a pot, and put the meat in the oil. Cook until a broth is formed. Cover until broth evaporates. Stir the meat for 5-10 minutes. Add salt, chili powder, garam masala, coriander powder, curry powder, and ginger and garlic pastes. Stir well. Add tomato puree and cook for 2-3 minutes. Add jalapeno peppers and garnish with coriander leaves.

Serve with rice or roti.

Meat Pilaf

I lb. meat (beef or lamb)
I lb. Basmati rice (washed)
2 potatoes (cut into 4 pieces each)
I medium onion (sliced)
7-8 cloves
3-4 Black peppercorns
3-4 green chili peppers
1 tsp. Garlic paste
1 tsp. Salt
1 cup oil
2 cinnamon stick
4 cardamom

Boil in separate pot, meat with ginger and garlic paste, cinnamon, cardamom, cloves and the grinded cloves, peppercorns, and chili peppers until tender. Fry in separate pot the sliced onion until it turns lightly golden brown then add potato and fry for one minute, take meat out of the mixture (from the first pot) and add to the fried potatoes and onions till it is golden brown then add the already washed rice and fry for a one minute and then add meat mixture with enough water to stand an inch above the rice and cook till the rice turns completely tender and dry. Remove.

Serve with garden salad and Riata.

Bombay Nan Chap

I lb. ground beef/lamb
3 tbsp. cuscus (finely ground)
2 tsp. cumin seeds, roasted and powdered
2 tsp. Ground fennel seeds (saunf)
I large onion
I tbsp. garlic paste
I tbsp. ginger paste big green chilies
tsp. Garam masala powder, all spices
1/4 tsp. Turmeric powder
1/2 a bunch coriander leaves, cilantro
I tsp. Papaya juice
1/4 cup oil half a lime
pinch of salt

Fry the onion in oil until light golden brown. Add the garlic and ginger pastes and fry for one minute. Add all the cumin, fennel, turmeric powder and cuscus. Add meat and papaya juice and salt. Let it cook on low heat until the meat is done. Add a little water if desired. Add green chilies and cook for five minutes. Sprinkle with garam masala powder and garnish with coriander leaves. Squeeze lime.

Serve with nan.

Tandoori Chicken

I chicken, whole
2 tsp. Cumin seeds
2 tsp. Chili powder
2 tsp. Garam masala powder (all spices)
2 tsp. Ginger paste
I tsp. Turmeric powder
I large onion, chopped
I cup yogurt
I tsp. Salt
1/4 cup oil

Mix all the above with yogurt in medium-sized bowl. Apply the yogurt masala on the whole chicken with a brush. Let the chicken marinate in the masala for one hour in the oven for one hour, until the meat separates from the bone. Garnish with coriander leaves and serve warm.

Egg and Potato Bhujia

2 eggs, blended
3 large potatoes, cut and sliced
I fresh tomato
I onion, sliced
I tsp. Chili powder (or 2 chopped green chilies)
¼ tsp. Turmeric powder I fresh tomato
½ tsp. Salt
3 tablespoons oil
tbsp. ginger and garlic paste tbsp. cumin seeds
Chopped cilantro

Fry onion until golden brown. Add cumin seeds, potatoes, and the rest of the ingredients. Cover and cook on low heat for ten minutes (steam cook). When tender, add blended eggs and cook for 3 minutes. Sprinkle coriander or cilantro to garnish.

Serve with roti or nan

Fried Cabbage

I medium sized cabbage, finely sliced
I onion
I tsp. Mustard seeds
4 -5 green chilies, chopped (or I tsp. of red chili pepper powder)
1/2 cup oil
½ tsp. salt
¼ tsp. turmeric powder

Heat oil, onion, and mustard seeds. When golden brown, add the rest
of the ingredients and cover.

Serve with rice or roti.

Besan Curry

2 cups gram flour
2 lb. plain yogurt
I small onion, chopped
I tsp. mustard seeds
I tsp. cumin seeds
1/2 tsp. fenugreek seeds
7-8 green chilies, sliced
¼ cup oil pinch of salt

Beat the yogurt. Mix the gram flour and about 3 cups of water slowly with the yogurt and stir to a fine paste. Fry the mustard and cumin seeds in oil.

Add the fenugreek seeds and fry. Add gram-yogurt mixture, onion, chilies, and salt. Stir for a few minutes, until moisture thickens. Put pakoras in this curry, if desired.

Spinach and Potato [Palak Paneer)

I lb. of spinach
4 potatoes cut and peeled (can be substituted with fried paneer)
3-4 green chili peppers
½ tsp. Salt
¼ tsp. Turmeric powder
I tsp. Cumin seeds
½ cup oil
I large onion, chopped
I tomato (or 2 tbsp. of tomato puree)

Fry onion in oil on medium heat. Add cumin and fry for I minute. Add all the rest of the ingredients and cover the pot. Cook for ten minutes until all the water evaporates and potatoes are tender.

Serve with Nan or Roti.

Egg Plant (Bangan Bhartha)

I eggplant-boiled or grilled, remove skin
I sliced onion
2-3 green chili peppers
½ tsp. Salt
2 tbsp. oil
½ tbsp. cumin
I large tomato

Fry onion and cumin until golden brown. Then add eggplant, salt, tomato, and pepper. Beat it with a wooden spoon, until it is mashed.

Serve hot with roti or chapatti.

Fried Okra (Bhindi)

One lb. fresh okra washed, chopped and dry large onion
tomato
½ cup fenugreek (Mithi) seeds
½ cup oil
pinch of turmeric powder
3 hot green peppers

Take a non-stick pan add 1/4 oil heat, add okra and fry in the oil until slight brown and when it is no longer sticky, set aside. On a separate saucepan take 1/4 oil, onions, and fenugreek seeds until golden brown. Then add the already fried okra, salt and pepper, tomato, and turmeric powder. Stir all these until dark brown. Sprinkle with freshly chopped coriander/cilantro leaves.

Serve with roti/ chapati

Omelet

6 eggs
I large onion, finely chopped
I green large pepper, finely chopped I large fresh tomato, finely
chopped ½ tsp. Salt
½ tsp. Black pepper
½ cup fresh coriander leaves I tbsp. oil

Beat eggs with a wire beater until well blended. Add all the ingredients
except the oil. Put a non-stick pan on medium heat and then add
the oil. When the oil is heated, put half of the egg mix onto the pan.
After two minutes, flip the eggs upside down. Let it cook slowly for
3-4 minutes, or until desired. Repeat with another half, if necessary.

Serve with paratha.

Roti

2 cup wheat flour
½ cup water pinch of salt

Mix all ingredients in a large bowl. Knead the dough. Add water gradually, if needed. Leave the dough standing for five minutes.

Make round balls and then flatten by using some dry flour, if sticky, into round patties. On a flat surface, using a dough roller roll into a thin round pancake type shape. Lift carefully from surface and place onto a hot flat pan. When it turns a shade darker than the original color tum the roti. Continue to do so until the roti turns a light brown color.

Serve with curry/vegetables

Fish in Garlic Sauce

I lb. fish fillet
5-6 garlic cloves, crushed
½ cup soft breadcrumbs
½ cup fish stock
3 tbsp. oil
I lemon

Heat oil in a pan. Add the fish and cook turning over for 6-8 minutes. Remove the fish in a plate. In the same pan, add garlic, squeeze lemon, and breadcrumbs. Cook until oil is fully absorbed. Add stock and simmer for 2-3 minutes. Pour sauce onto the fish.

Serve with boiled rice.

Salmon Steak

2Ibs Salmon steaks
½ pack Shan fish masala
¼ tsp. Salt
8 oz. Crushed tomato
I onion, chopped
I garlic clove, grated
¼ cup com oil
¼ cup fresh coriander leaves (or dry methi leaves)

Brown onions in oil and add washed steaks in a saucepan. Cover 3 minutes. Tum sides. Keep on medium heat for I minute, covered. Then uncover and remove the black skin from the steaks with a wooden spoon and fork. Return to saucepan. Sprinkle half of the ¼ of Shan masala mix and salt on fish. Add crushed tomato and grated garlic to masala mix. Cover I minute and then flip the steaks again. Sprinkle the other half of the Shan masala on the fish. Add fresh coriander leaves and cover. Prep time: 20 minutes.

Serve with boiled rice or garden salad.

DESSERTS

Sheer Khurma

One Gallon . milk
8 oz. Vermicelli
I lb. Sugar
2-3 Cardamom seeds
1 Cloves
8 oz. whipping cream Almonds
Pistachios
Oil--according to taste

Brown vermicelli in a little oil. Add milk and cook for IO minutes. Add sugar, cardamom, cloves and fine chopped pistachios and almonds. Cook for 3 minutes. Cool in freezer/fridge.

Mango Ice Cream

cup mango pulp
½ cup sugar
I can evaporate milk (chilled)

Mix all the above ingredients thoroughly and freeze until it begins to thicken. Remove from the freezer and whisk the mixture until its smooth. Then put it again in the freezer.

Banana Trifle

6 large ripe bananas
custard made with custard powder strawberry jam
cup whipping cream mixed nuts (chopped)

Prepare custard with custard powder according to the instructions on the package and keep ready.

Peel bananas and halve lengthwise. Spread one half of the banana slice with am and place the other half on top. Press together lightly and arrange in a glass dish. Pour the custard. Whip the cream to a stiff froth and pile over the trifle. Decorate with nuts and serve.

*You can also layer in different fruits and make a fruit trifle. Arrange in a glass dish so it will be visible.

Yellow Sweet Rice

(Zerda)

2 cups of rice
½ cup sugar
½ tsp. yellow food coloring
¼ cup oil
¼ cup raisin, nuts, almonds few seeds of cardamom
8 oz. whipping cream

Boil 6 cups of water and add the yellow colorant to it when rice is halfway done. Drain all the liquid and leave rice in the strainer. Heat up oil. Add cardamom, until the seeds become brownish. Add sugar and whipping cream. Mix it well. Add the rice into this mixture and stir once more, and nuts and raisins, if desired. Steam cook for five minutes-rice is done.

Serve after the main dish.

Gulab Jamun

A.
4 cups Carnation instant dry milk
I cup Crisco shortening
I cup flour
I cup milk
2 tsp. baking powder

B. Syrup
4 cups of sugar
4 cups of water
few seeds of cardamom

C.
Combine and cook on low heat for IO minutes and cool in fridge for
I 0 minutes.
2 cups of oil, for frying

Mix A. ingredients and form into small balls. Deep-fry the balls in oil
until golden brown. Put balls in the syrup.

Ras Malai

2 pints fresh whipping cream
I lb. ricotta cheese
½ cup sugar
I tbsp. rose water
I tbsp. kewra

Put ricotta cheese in a flat tray and place in oven at 300°F for I 5 minutes, or until it becomes hard and a slightly golden color. Cut ricotta cheese into small round slices. Beat the whipping cream with sugar, rose water and kewra for 2-4 minutes. Pour whipping cream mix onto ricotta cheese slices. Place in a deep freezer to cool down. Then place in the fridge. Serve cool.

Printed in the United States
by Baker & Taylor Publisher Services